T0194955

THE
MOST
IMPORTANT
THING

100 YEARS FROM NOW
NOTHING ELSE WILL MATTER

G. BOYCE CLAY

WESTBOW
PRESS®
A DIVISION OF THOMAS NELSON
& ZONDERVAN

WestBow Press books may be ordered through booksellers or by contacting:

WestBow Press
A Division of Thomas Nelson & Zondervan
1663 Liberty Drive
Bloomington, IN 47403
www.westbowpress.com
844-714-3454

Because of the dynamic nature of the Internet, any web addresses or links contained in
this book may have changed since publication and may no longer be valid. The views
expressed in this work are solely those of the author and do not necessarily reflect the
views of the publisher, and the publisher hereby disclaims any responsibility for them.

Any people depicted in stock imagery provided by Getty Images are models,
and such images are being used for illustrative purposes only.
Certain stock imagery © Getty Images.

ISBN: 978-1-6642-4001-8 (sc)
ISBN: 978-1-6642-4002-5 (hc)
ISBN: 978-1-6642-4000-1 (e)

Library of Congress Control Number: 2021914131

Print information available on the last page.

WestBow Press rev. date: 07/21/2021

DEDICATION

This book I here dedicate
To my God-given wife
Whose presence reminds me
That mine is . . .
"a Wonderful Life!"

"So we follow God's own Fool
For only the foolish can tell
Believe the unbelievable,
And come be a fool as well"[1]

---

[1] *God's Own Fool*, Michael Card, 1986

CONTENTS

FOREWORD

Perhaps the most enigmatic person in the Scriptures is the Apostle Peter. We live in a world where any singular misstep from your past can be used to discredit your viability and character. In such a world, Peter would be open to much destructive criticism. In this book, Dr. Gregory Clay introduces us to two Peters . . . a pre-conversion version and the second edition Peter who has experienced the Messiah and our Savior. The first edition was a brash and selfish reactionary individual. The second was a humble, unselfish, and charismatic devotee to The Way. This book describes both Peters and the transformation from one to the other. It also responds to the question, "What does that transformation look like?"

This book paints the two Peters with words from the Scripture. In Greg's Bible Classes, following a response from a student stating some basic characteristic of a believer derived from the Scripture, Greg usually replies with the question, "How does that look?" That is, how does that translate to behavior in life . . . in MY life. This book responds to that question concerning the transformation that occurs when one believes the words of Jesus and walks in His Way. Or, as Francis Schaeffer puts it, "How then should we live?"

We will see that this pursuit will be undergirded by understanding what the most important thing in this life is. Read the book to discover the answer to that question. The first two sections present a challenge and a foundation from which to launch your approach to that challenge. The challenge is to incorporate into your life and then energize that life by focusing on the most important thing in my daily walk.

The final section of the book is what that walk "looks like" in this alien world in its various parts and in relationships with different people of that world. You will note that each chapter begins with a narrative.

That narrative paints a word-picture of a real section of that world. That painting is representative of what "dying to the world and living for Christ" "looks like!" For the reader, it's the "What Now?" part of the book. The paintings are pictures of a transformed believer in an alien world! The Reader will be further challenged to discover what that looks like in their personal world.

Dr. Ernest Sturch, Jr.
Durant, Oklahoma
February, 2020

PREFACE

Dear Reader,

Thank you for accepting my invitation.

What invitation, you ask? Well, implicit on the cover and in the title of every book is an invitation to the curious to read. And when a reader turns back the cover of the book, he or she enters into the world of the author. So, it's only proper and fitting that you know something about the circumstances that brought about the writing of this book.

Everybody's got a book in them. My mentor[2] believes that each of us has only one . . . and that those who write more than one simply rework the same book over and over . . . but that's another story. Well, this is the one, and maybe the only one that's in me. But I believe that it is a book that God has been implanting in me moment by moment, day by day over the course of a lifetime. And before you start thinking that I'm something special, or even that I think that I'm something special, let me reassure you that I'm just a guy.

Just a regular guy[3].

But even if I am just a regular guy, when God calls you to do something,

---

[2] Dr. Ernest Sturch, Former Research Chemist, Oak Ridge National Laboratory; Retired Vice President for Instruction, Provost, Dean, Professor, Southeastern Oklahoma State University; Retired Minister, Bokchito Church of Christ, Bokchito, Oklahoma; Shepherd Emeritus, Park Avenue Church of Christ, Denison, Texas. Ernie and I have shared weekly breakfasts together since 1977.

[3] My thanks to Jeff Walling, Founding Director of the Youth Leadership Initiative at Pepperdine University. Jeff introduced me to the concept of "the guy" in a presentation at a youth rally in Tulsa in 1983. "The guy" was the servant of Elisha, whose eyes were opened to God's army of angels after Elisha's prayer. (II Kings 7)

I've found that it's not ever in your best interest to tell Him no, even if what He's asking of you doesn't make sense. Just ask Jonah.[4]

That same mentor reminds me that when God calls you to Nineveh, Satan will always have a ship waiting to take you to Tarshish. And while I may have delayed answering God's call to write this book, He just seemed to reinforce His call almost daily. And since I far prefer swallowing fish to being swallowed *by* fish . . .

So, yes, it's important to me that you understand that I'm just a regular guy. And I don't want that to come across as some sort of false humility. I hope that you understand that it's my desire to allow this book to illuminate The Book. My prayer is that the Holy Spirit will shine His light of understanding on this one little five-chapter letter we know as First Peter. For God inspired an unschooled fisherman to pen what I believe is the most revealing book in the New Testament.

God's words through Peter are inerrant; mine are not. God's words through Peter are infallible; mine are not. Peter's words are divinely inspired; mine are not.

To borrow from the greatest Christian mind of the twentieth century, "I am not trying to tell you in this book what I could do – I can do precious little – I am telling you what Christianity is. I did not invent it."[5]

The first seed for this book was planted when my mentor revealed some of the historical details surrounding the writing of First Peter. And God has used it to change my life. He used it to give me peace, joy, grace, purpose, direction, and "a place to stand."[6]

God then allowed me to watch First Peter change others as I taught it in a weekly high school/college class; it took eighteen months to cover just five chapters! Then I taught it in an adult class. Then I taught it again, and again, and again. It was in that teaching context that pearl after pearl of insight began to pour forth from Peter's letter. These insights were

---

[4] Jonah 1:1-3
[5] C.S. Lewis (1898-1963); *Mere Christianity*, p. 115
[6] Dr. D. Elton Trueblood (1900-1994); *A Place to Stand*

enhanced by pearls from other people in my life; hence, the abundant footnotes![7] And the more pearls I discovered, the more my life changed.

God hemmed me in[8] . . . and He wouldn't let me go.

Hence, **The Most Important Thing**. I couldn't *not* write it.

I would predict that this will not be a popular book, but still, I couldn't *not* write it. Not popular because Peter's message of Christ's calling is hard to accept. Bonhoeffer nailed it: "When Christ calls a man, He bids him come and die."[9] But the contrariety of Peter's message is that, with the calling comes the crown.

First Peter answers the Big Questions of life, the really deep questions:

Who am I?

Why am I here?

What is my purpose?

Does my life matter?

Who's in control?

What *does* it mean to be a Christian?

Through other questions . . . lots of questions, we'll explore God's revelation of meaning . . . of reality.

I expect that, as you read this book, there will be a surprise or two along the way. There certainly has been for me. There certainly was for Peter as his life took surprising turn after surprising turn, because . . .

God hemmed Peter in . . . and He wouldn't let him go.

God hemmed me in . . . and He wouldn't let me go.

So, as you read **The Most Important Thing**, as you explore the book of First Peter, see if God hems you in as well. Because if He does, He just may not let you go either.

---

[7] "What has been will be again, what has been done will be done again; there is nothing new under the sun. Is there anything of which one can say, 'Look! This is something new'? It was here long ago; it was here before our time." (Ecclesiastes 1:9-10, NIV)

[8] Psalm 139:5 (NIV)

[9] Dietrich Bonhoeffer (1906-1945) *"The Cost of Discipleship"*

ACKNOWLEDGMENTS

This book is the sum of every person who has touched my life. Some for a short period. Some for a lifetime. But each person left an imprint. Many are quoted. Some referenced. Some have their stories told. But a few must be specifically named . . . and thanks given.

To Doris Andrews, my Freshman English Composition professor at Southeastern Oklahoma State University. She took a group of "children of the sixties" and inspired them to use language not only to communicate, but to inspire others. That special summer class forged relationships that lasted lifetimes, and Doris was the catalyst. She was the spark and hers was the persistence that made this book happen. My regret is that Alzheimer's robbed my dear friend of the ability to see and appreciate the fruit of her labor so many years ago.

To my middlest daughter, Audrey Lynn Marie. Thank you so much for using your gift to bless your Papa. How thankful I am for that gift! And to my sister-in-law, Beverly Ann. These two English teachers served as wonderful editors. You took my bumblings and made them sound good.

To my "readers." What started as my "Dirty Dozen" grew to a cadre of friends and family brave enough to invest time in a total unknown. So, to family: Pam (my dearest), Nathan & Beth Anderson, Aaron & Audrey Loney, Drs. Scott & Stephanie Mendell, Dr. George & Beverly Hatfield; and friends: Bridget Youngblood, Todd Catteau, Basil McClure, Skip Clark, James Bird, Chris Slaughter, and Kevin Dale . . . you are the best guinea pigs!

To Kathy Sturch, who continued to encourage me to write, then to publish. She not only served as reader and gave of her time, but continued to push when I needed it. And to Cina Catteau, whose graphic gift condensed this book into a single image on its cover.

And to Ernie, my mentor. It would be hard for him not to see himself in this book. Much as I often seem to hear my father's voice coming out of my mouth at unexpected times, so one can see Ernie's words leaping from the pages of this book. There is no way to express the influence this mentor had on the life of his mentee. My only prayer is that of Elisha to Elijah, "Let me inherit a double portion of your spirit."[10] Here's to many more years of weekly breakfasts!

---

[10] II Kings 2:9 (NIV)

INTRODUCTION

"If we love ourselves and love money more than we love others,
we will get to a point where we will be more concerned about
our standard of living than we are about others living."[11]

I

"'Is this the day I die?'
Li Quan asked himself the familiar question
as he wiped sleep from his eyes."[12]

Is this the day I die? Not exactly an "upper" of a question with which to
begin a book, is it? Does it compel the reader to forge ahead? It's a question
that few of us ever ask until perhaps we're faced with a life-threatening
illness.

In Randy Alcorn's novel, *Safely Home*, the protagonist, Li Quan,
asked that question every morning. Living in China, a land where social,
economic, and physical persecution of Christians is an everyday reality, it's
a realistic question for a Christian to ask. Li knew that every day brought
with it the real possibility of death.

In our country, we really don't stop to ask that question. We focus on
living, on prolonging life. My generation (the Baby Boomers) thought we
were going to live forever. Death was something for others. Old people.
Those with debilitating illnesses. It was for self-destructive rock icons,

---

[11] Francis Chan, Author/Teacher/Pastor
[12] Randy Alcorn, *Safely Home*

members of the "27 Club"[13], like Jim Morrison, Janis Joplin, or Jimi Hendrix. Not us. We protested the Vietnam War because it was wrong for eighteen-year-olds to die. We were vibrant, optimistic, and immortal, "forever young"[14] . . . or so we thought. After all, "don't trust anyone over thirty"[15] we said (because we were never going to be "over thirty.") We "never wanna die."[16]

So, being forced to face the certainty of our mortality is not a popular message. Messages about death are not those that most of us wanted to hear.

We Baby Boomers fell into the all-too-human trap of Sir Thomas Browne: "The long habit of living indisposeth us for dying."[17] Or we aligned ourselves with one of our contemporaries, Woody Allen, "I'm not afraid of death. I just don't want to be there when it happens."

But we were fooled . . . and we were fools.

Now in our fifties, sixties, and seventies, we realize that death is a reality for all of us. Even rock icons who aren't self-destructive die: George Harrison, Glen Frey, Paul Revere, Mama Cass Elliot. The point finally comes when we realize that we have more yesterdays than tomorrows. As our grandparents, then parents die, we lose our "buffer", our "shield" between us and death.

So, sooner or later, regardless of our generation, the answer to that question (whether we ask it or not) will be yes. Today will be the day I die.

And in a country and in a culture that has become increasingly hostile to Christians, Li Quan's question takes on a new, more intense, and more focused meaning for those of us living in these United States.

Cardinal Francis George[18] predicted, "I expect to die in bed, my successor will die in prison, and his successor will die a martyr in the public square. His successor will pick up the shards of a ruined society and slowly help rebuild civilization, as the church has done so often in human history"

---

[13] Along with Rolling Stones founder Brian Jones, their deaths at age 27 prompted speculation of something mystical about the age of 27 and rock musicians.
[14] Bob Dylan, 1973
[15] Jack Weinberg (b. 1940), November, 1964
[16] Steppenwolf, "Born to be Wild", 1968
[17] Sir Thomas Browne (1605-1682) in *Hydriotaphia*, Urn Burial, Chapter V.
[18] 1937-2015; Archbishop of Chicago, 1997-2014; President of the United States Conference of Catholic Bishops from 2007 to 2010.

Then Cardinal George's thought and Li Quan's daily question spawn another and more indicting question: *"How* will I die?" Will it be in bed, in prison, as a martyr in the public square?

Thank God we don't have to wonder how to respond to those questions. Our brothers and sisters in the first century were asking the same questions. And Peter allows the Holy Spirit to answer not the specific questions, but how to deal with those questions . . . for them and for us.

So now *we* must begin to ask the question: "Is this the day I die?"

II

"I told them (Liena's two children), 'As long as God wants us to be safe, we will be safe, that He is in control . . . even in the bloodshed . . . during the killing . . . He is carrying our future. This is what it means to be a Christian in Syria.'

Am I a good mother, to have to tell my children such things?"[19]

To mark the 2014 International Day of Prayer for the Persecuted Church, Voice of the Martyrs published a YouTube video entitled "Liena's Prayer." In that video, Liena, a Christian mother living in the midst of the war in Syria, tells her story of having to inform her two children that they may have to face Muslims with swords asking them to recant their belief in Christ. She tells them that they may die and how they may die, but that they should not deny Jesus.

While those of us in the United States may not face such physical persecution yet, there can be no doubt that we live in a post-Christian society. No longer is it popular or safe to be a Christian. As I write this, societal persecution has been rampant for years, and economic persecution is ramping up quickly. Can physical persecution be far behind?

But regardless of which of Cardinal George's categories of death we may have before us, for now, we live. And that begs the question posed by the title of Dr. Francis Schaeffer's book and film series, "How Should We Then Live?"

And there, my friend, is the crux of Peter's letter. The important

---

[19] Liena's Prayer

question is not how we will die, but how we must live. How do we live counter to the hostile culture that we find ourselves living in?

"To live is Christ, and to die is gain," Paul wrote. (Philippians 1:21, NIV)

The YouTube video of *Liena's Prayer* ends with the statement "This is what it means to be a Christian in Syria" fading into the question without location, "Is this what it means to be a Christian?" In this letter, Peter not only deals with the questions about our death, but he makes clear what it means to be a Christian, what it means to live for Christ . . . in Rome, in Jerusalem, in Durant, Oklahoma or New York City . . . in the First Century, in the Twenty-first Century.

And the answer to both just may surprise you.

In fact, perhaps we could drill down to an even more basic question that will serve as the foundation for answering any other questions:

What's **the most important thing**?

Have you ever researched your genealogy? If so, you soon realize that, after going back two or three generations, you don't know much about these people at all. No one remembers; no one cares. So, one hundred years from now, what will anyone remember about you? What will have mattered in your life? For your time on this planet . . .

What's **the most important thing**?

I invite you to come with me on a journey through this little letter. It's only five chapters long. But within those short five chapters, Peter reveals some things that just may change your life . . . and your death.

III

I've divided this book into three sections.

After setting the stage in the first section, the second section deals with our calling, our mission, the "why." It tells us why to live, why we're here. It calls on us to recall our true home and the foreign nature of this world. Understanding of this section is essential to living out the final section.

That third section tells us the "how." How to live, how to model Jesus to the world that we've been called to save.

Along the way, you'll meet some folks who have lived out Peter's call. Some of them are my heroes.

This is a book study, an expository study of a 2000-year-old letter. But it's more. This is a character study of a guy, a man, an ordinary man who underwent an extraordinary transformation.

SECTION ONE

PROLOGUE

"One more day . . . one less day . . ."[20]

It began as a day like any other day in Capernaum.

Simon was with his brother Andrew, and his business partners, James and John. (He called the two of them "the Thunder Brothers.") They went fishing. Whether it was in the shallows of the lake or from their boat in the deep, each day was the same. The routine was certain; only the outcome was in doubt. Cast nets . . . catch fish . . . clean nets . . . repeat.

But this day would not end like any other. A man from across the hills named Yeshua would call Simon and his friends to leave their routine and join His adventure. Little did Simon know . . .

This day would end with him in the presence of God.

Another day, three years later. Everything had changed. Nothing was certain. Nothing was routine. Simon was now Peter. The adventure seemed to be over. He and his companions were in Jerusalem, a long way from home. Their King was gone. His final instructions? Wait. Ten days had passed since they last saw Him disappear into the clouds. What now? Little did Peter know . . .

This day would end with the presence of God *in him*.

Two days. One, a day of calling; the other, the Day of Pentecost. Two days that were so different. Two days that changed the direction, the purpose, the outcome of one man's life. Two days that were days of definition for Simon Peter.

The days were different . . . and so was Peter.

---

[20] Dr. Bill Brown, Senior Fellow of Worldview and Culture and Dean of the Colson Fellows Program at the Colson Center for Christian Worldview. Former President of Cedarville University and Bryan College.

ONE

THE CALL

"We're not citizens of earth trying to get to heaven.
We're citizens of heaven sojourning here on earth."[21]

---

[21] Dr. Adrian Rogers (1931-2005), Pastor, Bellevue Baptist Church, Memphis, Tennessee, 1972-2005; Three-term President, Southern Baptist Convention

THE MOST IMPORTANT THING | 1

"Space . . . the final frontier . . ."

So began Captain James T. Kirk's account of "the voyages of the Starship Enterprise. Its continuing mission: to explore strange new worlds, to seek out new life and new civilizations, to boldly go where no man has gone before."[22]

And so similarly begins the Holy Spirit's account of <u>our</u> "continuing mission" in our brother Peter's first letter. He wrote to Christians as "strangers in the world," "aliens," "chosen . . . that you may declare the praises of Him who called you out of darkness into His wonderful light." Not only that, He tells us, His "Holy nation," to have "no fear" even though we "may have had to suffer grief in all kinds of trials."

So how is it that we are to live in a world that is not home to us? How do we function on a hostile planet? How do we behave, we who are "twice-born in a once-born world" (as Dr. Rogers calls us)? We are, after all, well . . . different, aren't we? And if so, how are we different? And why? What is my purpose? Why was I born? Do I really matter? Does my life really make a difference? *Should* my life really make a difference? What does it mean to be a Christian?

Wow . . . lots of questions, huh? Really deep questions.

Fortunately, God gave us First Peter. This little book near the end of the Bible gives some incredible answers to these and tons of other questions. Questions that cut to the heart of life. Questions that can change a life . . . my life . . . your life.

So, let's cut to the chase.

Spoiler alert.

This book is about selflessness.

Pure, unadulterated, selflessness.

First.

Last.

Always. In every situation.

Even to the giving of your life.

Peter says it. Paul says it in every one of his letters. Jesus says it. Jesus lived it. Jesus died it . . . on the cross.

---

[22] *Star Trek* (the original television series, 1966-1969)

Charles Spurgeon[23] once counseled regarding preaching that "I take my text and make a beeline to the cross." Peter's text is all about the cross. And the cross is all about selflessness, sacrifice, and surrender of the will.

This is not rocket science. It's not brain surgery. Well, maybe it is in some way a type of brain surgery. At least (to paraphrase Paul) Peter may transform us *by the renewing of our minds.*[24] The fact is . . .

You're selfish.

I don't even know you, but I can make that statement. Selflessness does not come naturally. Our flesh is selfish. It's sinful. We were born selfish. We inherited it from our father, Adam. And it takes brain surgery to change it.[25]

I like the way my friend, Mitch Wilburn[26], says it:

"Jesus came:

not to change your diet, but to change your appetite,
not to change your conduct, but to change your character,
not to change what I do, but to change what I want to do."

We humans can't be forced to be selfless. That's the failing of socialism and communism. But Jesus can change the human heart to *want* to be selfless, even to the point of giving all, to the giving of one's life. *There* is the "brain surgery", the mind renewing that Paul speaks of.[27] And Peter provides the instruments to do the surgery. First Peter allows us to see both sides of the veil:

"The reason you can keep the particular is because you know the general. The reason you keep the finite is you know the infinite. The reason you can do the lower story is you know the upper story."[28]

---

[23] 1834-1892

[24] Romans 12:2

[25] In fact, it may take brain surgery on you to keep you from confusing the two words as you encounter them in this book: self*ish*ness vs. self*less*ness . . . Antonyms! Opposites! Watch! Beware!

[26] Preaching Minister, Park Plaza Church of Christ, Tulsa, Oklahoma.

[27] Romans 12:2

[28] Tommy Nelson, Senior Pastor, Denton Bible Church, *Song of Solomon*

Roy O. Disney[29] helps us even more: "When your values are clear to you, making decisions becomes easier." I've condensed it slightly to this mantra: Decisions are easy when values are clear.

If you're like me, there are big (and sometimes small) decisions that come up in your life. Where to live. Who to marry. What career to choose or what job to take. What church to attend. And at some point, you wind up saying (or at least thinking) these words: "Man, I'm really *struggling* with this decision." You're conflicted. One minute, you lean one way. One day, you lean another. But you're still mush. You toss and turn at night. You wait and wait for clarity.

Hopefully, you seek God for the answer. You pray. You read. You meditate. You seek Godly counsel. But the answer eludes you.

I would submit that the answer lies in your ability and my ability to define our values, to make them clear. There is no struggle when we are clear on our values. Decisions are easy when values are clear.

And Jesus' highest value is clear: It's selflessness . . . the selflessness of the cross. So, let's dive into First Peter and see how and why this is His highest value . . . why this is so, well . . . Jesus.

---

[29] 1893-1971, Co-founder with his brother, Walt, of The Disney Company

??? QUESTIONS FOR REFLECTION

- How is it that we are to live in a world that is not home to us? How do we function on a hostile planet? How do we behave, we who are "twice-born in a once-born world"?
- How are we different? And why?
- What is my purpose? Why was I born?
- Do I really matter? Does my life really make a difference?
- *Should* my life really make a difference?
- What does it mean to wear the name of Christ? To be a Christian?

TWO

THE CONDITIONS

I Peter 1:1a, 5:13

"Enemy-occupied territory . . . that is what this world is."[30]

---

[30] C. S. Lewis, *Mere Christianity*, 1952

·· 2 ··

A man leaves home. When he gets to the first corner, he turns left. When he gets to the next corner, he turns left. And when he gets to the next corner, he turns left again. When he gets home, there are two people there wearing masks. Who are they?

"There are three cardinal rules for studying Scripture[31]:

1. Context
2. Context
3. Context"

One of the valuable lessons that I've learned about studying scripture was taught by many teachers. But Dr. Money was perhaps the first to articulate to me those three cardinal rules.

The fact is, that those rules apply in a variety of arenas. Take the story above, for example. It's called a "story with a hole." There's one piece of information that's missing that will make the answer to the question evident to anyone in our culture. It will provide **context**, without which the story makes little sense, making the answer elusive. However, asking just the right question immediately solves the puzzle.

So before we dive off into the deep end of First Peter, it will help to have three contextual concepts (keeping in line with Dr. Money's three cardinal rules), some bits of information that will shine a bright light on these scriptural passages that give us so much powerful, life-changing information. Two are in the first verse, one in the next-to-the-last.

First, the author.

Second, the source.

Third, the circumstances.

---

[31] Dr. Royce Money, Former President, Chancellor, Abilene Christian University.

The Author

"Peter, an apostle of Jesus Christ . . ."

Most of us have some vague notion of who Peter was. We may remember that he denied Jesus three times. We may know that he walked on water with Jesus (then sank!), or that he was a fisherman. Some may know of his confession that "Jesus is the Christ, the Son of the living God," (Matthew 16:16, NIV) or that Jesus directed "Get thee behind me, Satan" (Matthew 16:23, KJV) to Peter.

Since verse one identifies the author as Peter, it might be a good idea to know something about who the author was. Without getting too far off into the weeds, it is imperative that we make a contrast between two Peters: pre-Pentecost . . . and post-Pentecost.

Peter's given name was Simon, but Jesus gave him a name that was both descriptive and challenging: Rocky. (In the Greek, Simon became *Petros*, which means "rock.") Pre-Pentecost, the name was challenging, and Peter was rarely up to the challenge. But post-Pentecost, Simon became the rock, "Rocky", and it became a descriptive.

Let's look at Peter before the Holy Spirit anointed him and the other Disciples on Pentecost. We'll just cite a few examples:

- "How many times shall I forgive?" (Matthew 18:21ff, NIV)
- "What about us?" (Matthew 19:27ff, NIV)
- "Not just my feet but my hands and my head as well!" (John 13:6ff, NIV)
- Cut off the ear of the high priest's servant. (John 18:10)
- Denied knowing Jesus three times. (Luke 22:54ff)
- Disappeared during Jesus' crucifixion. (Matthew 26:56b, John 19:25-27)

In each of these specific examples, Peter had only one thing in mind: self. Peter wanted only what was best for Peter. He (and the other disciples) believed that Jesus was going to be an earthly king, re-establishing the Israelite kingdom (a la Saul, David, and Solomon) on earth. And Peter wanted to be right there at the king's side, in the circle of power. He wanted the power and the authority that came with the power and authority of the king. It was all about Peter. Pure, fleshly selfishness.

Now, let's contrast that Peter with the post-Pentecost Peter:

- Preached with power and authority on the Day of Pentecost. (Acts 2:1-41)
- Before the Sanhedrin with courage. (Acts 4:1-22)
- "We must obey God rather than men." (Acts 5:42, NIV)
- "Who was I to think that I could oppose God?" (Acts 11:1-18, NIV)
- Jailbreak! (via an angel). (Acts 12:1-19)

In each of these pictures that we're given of Peter after receiving the Holy Spirit, he puts himself in harm's way. The selfish pre-Pentecost Peter becomes the self*less* post-Pentecost Peter who willingly gives of himself. His life becomes nothing. Tradition tells us that Peter indeed lost his life by crucifixion (upside down).

There's another way to look at it, perhaps a more "scientific" way.

When faced with stress, e.g. persecution, the body responds in a certain way. It's called the "fight or flight response." The sympathetic (or adrenergic) nervous system kicks into gear. Adrenaline or norepinephrine is released, preparing the body for action.

Pre-Pentecost, Peter responds with both.

In the Garden, he fights, pulls his sword, and cuts off the ear of Malchus. Fight.

That same night, at Jesus's trial, he flees, denies Jesus three times, not to be seen again until after the resurrection.

Post-Pentecost, he responds with neither.

As we get into the text of First Peter, remember who it is that writes the words. The Holy Spirit used Peter . . . all of him, his foibles as well as his strengths, pre-Pentecost and post-Pentecost, to show us the nature of God. One of the beauties of the Bible is that it doesn't minimize or hide the weaknesses of the characters chronicled. On the contrary, it uses them to point to the power and grace of the Creator God. Shakespeare had Marc Antony saying it like this:

"The evil that men do lives after them,
The good is oft interred with their bones."[32]

"Oft interred", maybe . . . but not always. In the case of Peter, the Holy Spirit used the contrast of the same man to allow us to see what he was like both before and after receiving the Holy Spirit. And that helps us to gain even more insight into the letter.

So, what made the difference between Peter pre-Pentecost and Peter post-Pentecost?

Pre-Pentecost, the Messiah cajoled.

Post-Pentecost, the Holy Spirit controlled.

Simon, the fisherman, became Peter (Rocky), the fisher *of* men.

One thing that I love about Jesus is that He doesn't give folks a personality transplant when He comes to live in them. Peter has most often been described as "impetuous", an accurate and well-deserved description. He was the kind of guy who would shoot first, and sort out the bodies later! Just ask Malchus, the high priest's servant who lost an ear thanks to Peter! (I suspect that a fisherman was not quite an accurate enough swordsman to actually intend to cut off only his ear. Fortunately for Malchus, I also suspect that he dodged and only lost his ear, not his head!)

So, as we look at the text, don't mistake personality with nature. God changes the latter without messing with the former.

The Source

Jesus provided the clarity, in His words and in His life, death, and resurrection. The Holy Spirit spoke through the New Testament writers to illuminate those values. But there are two categories of writers used by the Spirit in the New Testament.

The gospel writers (Matthew, Mark, Luke and John) tell us all about Jesus. We get the details of His life as they chronicle them. What He did. Where He went. Who He interacted with.

The gospel writers tell us what Jesus said. We can know *exactly* what Jesus said. In most editions of Scripture, we place importance on Jesus'

---

[32] Antony to Roman citizens, *Julius Caesar*, Act 3, Scene 2, William Shakespeare

words by highlighting them in red. And through the words of the four gospels, we can know about Jesus.

Verse one expands our identity of the author as "an apostle." So what's so special about the writings of the apostles as contrasted to the gospel chroniclers? Through the apostles, we get a chance to see what ordinary men *understood* Jesus to be about. What they understood about the life of Jesus, the words of Jesus, the death of Jesus. We get to see one degree of separation from Jesus. They walked and talked with him for three and a half years. Yet, at the ascension of Jesus, it's clear that the apostles still don't get it. They ask, "Lord, are you at this time going to restore the kingdom to Israel?" (Acts 1:6, NIV) They were still looking to the power provided by an earthly kingdom, with them as the power brokers of King Jesus.

On the day of Pentecost, the Holy Spirit made it all clear. The apostles finally understood. Their eyes widened, their wrinkled brows disappeared, and the corners of their mouths turned upward. Only then did they get it. It was their "Aha moment." It took what seemed to be tongues of fire resting on them, but they finally got it. And the spokesman, the one who penned the book we're about to explore, got it.

And there it is; one of the many things that make First Peter so special. Through the eyes of Peter, we get to see and hear from one like us.

Just a regular guy.

An ordinary, unschooled man (according to the Sanhedrin[33]), who had been with Jesus.

The Circumstances

The best scholarship tells us that this letter was written from Rome. Peter signs off the letter in the next-to-the-last verse with the salutation: "She who is in Babylon, chosen together with you, sends you her greetings . . ." (I Peter 5:13, NIV) and most scholars agree that "Babylon" is code for Rome (as it is in Revelation). If this is true, then certain shades begin to color this letter.

Since most scholars also date the letter in the sixties (A.D)[34], it would

---

[33] Acts 4:13

[34] This parenthetical notation is necessary for my fellow Boomers raised in the 1960s. As my mentor often chides me, we seem to think and act as if Western Civilization began with the Beatles.

most likely place Nero on the throne of the Roman Empire. He also ruled when Peter was executed in the late sixties. Nero's atrocities against Christians are well known. He not only blamed them for the burning of Rome, but often used fire to kill them, famously using them as human torches to light his gardens.

Once again, this background only heightens the level of selflessness that Peter exemplifies and to which he calls his first century brethren (and us). This also serves to further seal our ability to identify with Peter and the initial recipients of the letter as we face increasing persecution. And it's better to know these things as we begin rather than wait until the end of the letter.

Really, we don't care about who Peter was, where he was, who he wrote to, or any other details surrounding this book unless it helps us answer the big questions we talked about earlier.

So, if you haven't already, grab your Bible (paper or digital). Now, stop reading this book and read First Peter.

That's right. I'm asking you, encouraging you, to stop reading this book and read The Book.

It should take you about twelve minutes. (That's a good, perfect, Biblical number!) But now that you have some background, those twelve minutes should reveal some things that maybe you didn't see the first time you read the letter all the way through (if indeed you've ever actually read it all the way through). And with that reading, now maybe God will illuminate some of the things He wants to reveal to you the way He revealed them to me.

Just watch as we get into the text.

From here forward, I encourage you to keep your Bible open next to this book. At the beginning of each of the chapters of this book, I've posted the section of First Peter that we'll be talking about in that chapter. I pray that it will be easy for you to read and study the text of First Peter alongside this book.

Oh. The key contextual question for our introductory "story with a hole?" Where is home? The answer: on a baseball diamond. The two people wearing masks are the umpire and the catcher.

?!? QUESTIONS FOR REFLECTION

- Had you read the entire letter of First Peter in one sitting before today?
- How did the contextual concepts in this chapter change your understanding or your view of First Peter? Did you read it with new eyes this time?
- Living in the 21st century, do you have any sense of persecution?

SECTION TWO

THREE

THE MISSION

I Peter 1:1b

"You intended to harm me, but God intended it for
good to accomplish what is now being done, the
saving of many lives." (Genesis 50:20, NIV)[35]

---

[35] Joseph

In 2006, Henriann Catteau travelled to China with her father, Tom Goodwyn, to complete the adoption of Shen, the second son to be adopted from China by Henriann and her husband, Todd[36]. Shen was the best friend of Bao, adopted a year earlier, and would join the Catteau's biological daughters, Melanie and Cina. On their arrival, they met Bruce Chen, a twenty-three-year-old who had helped them with translating some documentation. What they didn't know was that Bruce was a Christian.

As they visited with Bruce over a meal, they quickly learned that Bruce's commitment to Christ had cost him . . . dearly. He had been cut off by his family. He received no financial support. He had been fired from four jobs for proselytizing on the job. He had been jailed. He was under surveillance. Even sharing this information in a public restaurant made the Catteau's primary translator nervous.

But when encouraged by Tom, a businessman, to tone down his rhetoric, Bruce said, "I can't stop preaching. I'm ready to die for Jesus."

One of the great things about Scripture is that God has preserved it for you and me. In the case of the New Testament, He's kept it for us for nearly two millennia. As we'll find from this look at First Peter, the message and the meaning are as fresh as today's text or tomorrow's Tweet.

God meant it for you. For me. For today.

But the original audience was more specific. And knowing and understanding that specificity also sheds more light on the message of I Peter. I like the way the ESV translates it:

"To those who are elect exiles of the dispersion . . ." (I Peter 1:1, ESV)

The Greek word for dispersion is *diaspora*, and it is most often thought of in terms of the "scattering" of the Jews throughout the world during Old Testament times. But in Acts 8, after Stephen's martyrdom, ". . . all except the apostles were scattered throughout Judea and Samaria." (Acts 8:1, NIV) It's often called "the Christian Diaspora." And the same nationalities mentioned here in First Peter were mentioned as having been in Jerusalem on the Day of Pentecost.[37]

---

[36] Preaching Minister, Park Avenue Church of Christ, Denison, Texas, 1994-Present
[37] Acts 2:8-10

The Jewish Diaspora was all about judgement and punishment.[38] God drove the Jews from the Promised Land because of their idolatry. But this dispersion, this Christian Diaspora, had a different purpose. It was about blessing! God's kingdom now has no borders! God drove the believers out of the warmth of the womb in Jerusalem. The birthplace of Christianity provided advantages, but it prevented the spread of the Gospel. So, God dispersed them from that womb, sending them to a strange land, in a strange culture, so "that the world may know"[39] about its Savior.

This scattering was about the saving of more souls.

Two thousand years later, our message is the same.

God has blessed me with the most beautiful wife in the world who loved Jesus before she loved me. And He has blessed us with three of the most beautiful, Godly daughters we could ever have imagined. He answered our lifelong prayers for our girls, and gave them each their perfect match: Godly husbands who love them second only to Jesus. He then poured further blessings out on us and has given us seven grandchildren. (Another good, Biblically complete number!)

Every time my family is together for a meal (which totals about three or four times each year), before we ask the blessing for God's provision, I remind the "Clamily" of something. I remind them that "the most important thing is that I see you on the other side. One hundred years from now, nothing else will matter."[40] As of this writing, I'm assured of seeing all of our daughters and sons-in-laws, along with the three oldest granddaughters, who were baptized together on September 8, 2013.

Four times in this letter, Peter drives home the mission.[41]

So, there you have it . . .

---

[38] Jeremiah 9:12-16
[39] Wonderful video series by Ray Vander Laan
[40] I'm indebted to Dr. James Dobson for inculcating this thought, phrase, and concept into my mind years ago.
[41] I Peter 1:7, 2:12, 3:1, 3:15-16

The.

Most.

Important.

Thing . . .

. . . is that I see the person God has put in front of me on
the other side. One hundred years from now . . .

Nothing.

Else.

Will.

Matter.

That was the message of the first century recipients. *This* is the message of the twenty-first century recipients.

So, who are the recipients? Us!

And who are we?

Ah, another story (an important one) for another chapter.

⁇ QUESTIONS FOR REFLECTION

- Is Bruce Chen a fool for not shutting up? Is he failing to be "wise as a serpent"? (Matthew 10:16, NIV) Or is he simply following Peter's example?[42]
- What is your purpose for being? Your mission?
- Is my mission specific for me? Or is it the same as for all others who have ever lived or will live after me?
- Are you ready to die for Jesus?
- Are you willing to live for Jesus?

---

[42] Acts 5:12-42

FOUR

THE COST

I Peter 1:1b

"The only hope you have is to accept the fact that you're already dead. The sooner you accept that, the sooner you'll be able to function as a soldier is supposed to function."[43]

---

[43] Captain Ronald Speirs, *Band of Brothers*

·· 4 ··

Imagine . . .

You receive a call from NASA. You've been selected, called for a special mission to a distant galaxy. Your mission: to save a dying civilization.

This civilization is advanced. Computers beyond your imagination. Communication is instantaneous. Travel on the planet and beyond is unlimited. There is little poverty, plenty of food. The planet is like a garden.

But, this civilization is barbaric. There is no absolute truth; each person makes up their own. Lying is the norm. Child sacrifice is common. Sex is the ultimate pursuit; tolerance the ultimate value. Murder is commonplace. The civilization seems to be totally selfish.

And the civilization is dying. There is a virus, a fatal disease that has doomed the culture.

But you have the cure. It must be taken daily, but it will produce a total cure.

However, there are side effects. There will be cerebral changes, a total change in character. These creatures will no longer have the desire to lie, or steal. No more willingness to commit murder or adultery. They will become totally self*less*.

Previous missions have failed. All members of the squadrons have died. Some became afflicted with the virus; some were murdered.

So? Would you go?

If you decided to go, how would you feel about home/earth?

How would you approach the people?

How would you relate to the rest of the crew?

Well, if you have claimed Jesus as your Savior, if you have named Him as your King, then I've just described you. Because here's how Peter addresses us:

". . . God's elect, strangers in the world . . ." (I Peter 1:1, NIV) Three times in this letter, Peter calls us strangers;[44] and in chapter two, he adds the descriptive "aliens."[45]

---

[44] 1:1, 1:17, 2:11

[45] 2:11

We just don't think of it that way, do we? We tend to think of earth as home. We are, after all, earthlings. Or, are we?

"We aren't meant for this life. We're passing through the land of the dying into the land of the living."[46]

Country singer Jim Reeves put a little folksier spin on it in this 1962 song:

This World Is Not My Home[47]
This world is not my home
I'm just a-passing through
My treasures are laid up
Somewhere beyond the blue.

The angels beckon me
From heaven's open door
And I can't feel at home
In this world anymore.

Peter addresses his first century recipients (and us as believers in the twenty-first century) not as we are, but as he wants us to be: not of this world. Remember? It's part of Paul's "renewing of the mind."[48]

But then Peter distinguishes us even further. He uses more descriptives to let us know that we're not just here. We're not simply marking time and occupying space until we get to go back home. Oh, no. We're on a mission: he refers to us as the "elect";[49] three times, he calls us chosen;[50] five times, he refers to us as "called";[51] and four times, he refers to us as "holy"[52]. Being holy even heightens the space analogy because its meaning is "set apart for a specific purpose."

And, like the crew of a spaceship must obey their commander as part

---

46 Carolyn McCulley "Pilgrims Passing Through" *World, November 1, 2014*
47 "This World Is Not My Home", Jim Reeves, 1962
48 Romans 12:2
49 1:1
50 1:2, 2:9, 5:13
51 1:15, 2:9, 2:21, 3:9, 5:10
52 1:15, 1:16, 2:5, 2:9

of their commission, we must obey our Commander.[53] This is our calling: obedience. And obedience is critical, whether to God, a commander, or a parent. Listen to one parent's response to her grown son's request for advice in child raising:

"As **self-will is the root of all sin and misery**, so whatever cherishes this in children ensures their after-wretchedness and irreligion; whatever checks and mortifies it promotes their future happiness and piety. This is still more evident, if we farther consider, that **religion is nothing else than doing the will of God, and not our own**: that the one grand impediment to our temporal and eternal happiness being this self-will, no indulgences of it can be trivial, no denial unprofitable. Heaven or hell depends on this alone. So that the parent who studies to subdue it in his child, works together with God in the renewing and saving a soul. The parent who indulges it does the devil's work, makes religion impracticable, salvation unattainable; and does all that in him lies to damn his child, soul and body forever."[54]

Ironic, isn't it? This wise mother knew that indulging a child's desire actually prevented them from securing what they really wanted: happiness. That denying what the child thought was "good" would actually result in something far better.[55] Her experience had taught her that to eschew the immediate would reward the eternal. That today's gratification denies tomorrow's joy.

Her words from the eighteenth century may ring harsh in our twenty-first century ears, but this wasn't so much a "breaking" of the will as it was a "redirecting" of the will, away from "my will be done" and toward "Thy will be done."

Susanna's key? Obedience.

And, like the crew of a spaceship, we will be trained.[56]

---

[53] 1:2b . . . our King, Jesus Christ
[54] Susanna Wesley (Mother of John & Charles)
[55] My mentor says, "Never let the good things in life rob you of the best."
[56] "sanctifying work of the Spirit"

And, like the crew of a spaceship, there will be a reward.[57] In our case, a gift; this is our crown.

We are on a mission . . . to save a dying world.

But how, you ask?

Keep reading.

---

[57] "sprinkling by His blood" This obscure reference eluded me for years, but is, in fact, rich with meaning and symbolism that Peter's Jewish readers would have readily understood. First, it represents the covenantal joining with God, vowing obedience to Him. (Exodus 24:4-8) Second, it pictures Jesus' once-and-for-all blood shed to give us the crown. (Hebrews 9:11-14, 18-28) So both obedience and reward shine brightly in this imagery. Both this world and the next are seen.

⁇ QUESTIONS FOR REFLECTION

- If I'm not different (in my behavior) from the world I'm living in, does that mean that the world is behaving like Jesus would, or am I behaving like the world does?
- If I'm not being persecuted (or at least ridiculed), am I fulfilling my mission?
- If I'm not undergoing suffering, am I accomplishing my purpose?
- Is Susanna Wesley overstating the case: ". . . **religion is nothing else than doing the will of God, and not our own**: that the one grand impediment to our temporal and eternal happiness being this self-will, no indulgences of it can be trivial, no denial unprofitable. Heaven or hell depends on this alone."

FIVE

THE REVELATION

I Peter 1:3-9

"Tribulation is the appointed path to the Kingdom,
and the only way you can get to the Kingdom is in the
patience of Christ. There are trials and sufferings on
that road, and no one ever finally escapes them."[58]

---

[58] Sir Walter Scott (1771-1832)

·· 5 ··

Ernest Gordon's story of captivity by the Japanese during World War II fills an entire book[59]. Two movies have chronicled those incredible days in Burma[60]. But one episode changed the captives. Gordon tells it:

One day a shovel is missing. The officer in charge becomes angry and demands that the missing shovel be produced or he will kill them all. No one budges until finally, one man steps forward. The officer beats the man to death. At the next tool check, there is no shovel missing and the men realize that there had been a miscount at the first check point. The prisoners are stunned. An innocent man was willing to die to save everyone else.

Peter is so good. He doesn't just throw us out there and let us flail around with no direction. He doesn't just tell us that we have a mission and then give us no tools with which to accomplish that mission, especially as daunting a mission as saving a dying world!

How do we save a dying world?

And the "how" answer to the mission is really pretty simple. It's not a matter of *what we do* as it is a matter of *who we are*.

Peter gives one of Scripture's great doxologies in verses three through five of the first chapter. One of my previous preaching ministers[61] committed this to memory and used it often, not only for its beauty, but for its comprehensiveness.

> "Praise be to the God and Father of our Lord Jesus Christ! In His great mercy He has given us new birth into a living hope through the resurrection of Jesus Christ from the dead, and into an inheritance that can never perish, spoil, or fade – kept in heaven for you, who through faith are shielded by God's power until the coming of the salvation that is ready to be revealed in the last time."

---

[59] *Miracle on the River Kwai*

[60] *Bridge On the River Kwai* (1957), *To End All Wars* (2001)

[61] Van C. Ledbetter (1934-2016); Van committed large portions of the New Testament (KJV) to memory and could quote them on command. I Peter 1:3-5 was his favorite passage.

Peter then calls his readers to join him in rejoicing in God's greatness, goodness, and grace because they are suffering "in all kinds of trials."[62]

Let's stop for a minute to recall and reflect on what "kinds of trials" our first century brethren were undergoing. We've already referred to the persecution at the hands of Nero. Peter knew full well how horrible that persecution was. It's entirely possible that Peter could smell the burning flesh of men, women, and children as they were rolled in oil and lifted on stakes to light Nero's garden in Rome at night. He may have heard the roar of the crowd in the Colosseum as lions tore into his brothers and sisters. And he knew that the persecution of those who had been scattered was equally horrifying. That persecution came from both the Jews and the Romans.

This raises a critical question.

Why didn't Peter just tell folks to "get outta' Dodge?"

Why didn't he just tell them to flee the persecution, the bloodshed, the pain, the suffering, the death? Why not just tell everybody to head for the hills? Why not holler, "Run for your lives?" Why not just say, "If these folks don't like us, let's just leave?"

Or, on the other hand, why not fight? Why not resist? Why not rebel? Granted, the forces of the Romans, and the religious and political power of the Jews were overpowering, but at least, why not go down fighting?

After all, wasn't Peter a master of "fight or flight?"

I mean, wasn't this the man who had the sword in the Garden?[63] Wasn't this the man who cut off the ear of the High Priest's servant[64] . . . against formidable odds?[65] Wasn't this the man who vowed that he would follow Jesus even if all fall away?[66] Even to prison?[67] Even to the death?[68]

And wasn't this the man who denied Jesus?[69] Not once? Not twice? But three times? With curses?[70] Wasn't this the man who fled from the scene

---

[62] 1:6

[63] John 18:10

[64] John 18:10

[65] John 18:3

[66] Matthew 26:33; Mark 14:29

[67] Luke 22:33

[68] Matthew 26:35; Mark 14:31; Luke 22:33; John 13:37

[69] Matthew 26:69-75; Mark 14:66-72; Luke 22:55-62; John 18:16-18, 25-27

[70] Matthew 26:74; Mark 14:71

of his Rabbi's trial?[71] Wasn't this the man who hid in fear of the Romans while that Rabbi was executed?

Peter was, indeed, a master of fight or flight.

Well, yes . . . but the operative root of the descriptor here is "was."

That is, that's who Peter *was*.

That was Peter before Pentecost. The man writing this letter isn't the Peter before Pentecost. It's the Peter after Pentecost. He's different. He's changed, or rather, Someone changed him. At Pentecost, the Holy Spirit revealed to Peter what he's now revealing to us.

And what is he revealing? That "fight or flight" is no longer the order of the day. Our flesh is not what rules anymore. That his adrenergic nervous system no longer determines his behavior (or ours). Something else is in control here. Or better said, Some_one_ else is in control. Someone who rules differently, and whose rules are different. Listen to that Someone:

"My kingdom is not of this world. If My kingdom were of this world, then My servants would be fighting so that I would not be handed over to the Jews; but as it is, My kingdom is not of this realm." (John 18:36, NASB)

Peter then tells them (and us) why the trials and suffering come: ". . . so that your faith . . . may result in praise, glory, and honor when Jesus Christ is revealed." (I Peter 1:7, NIV)

So, when is Jesus revealed?

For most of my life, I assumed that the time "when Jesus would be revealed" always referred to the Second Coming. And it does. But it also refers to Jesus being revealed *to* others *through* the believers. As the Holy Spirit sanctifies us day by day, minute by minute, Jesus is revealed to others by our actions as we imitate Him.

My selfless actions, my sacrificial acts, these display Jesus to others. And in turn, my life results in praise, glory, and honor . . . not to me, but to Jesus Christ. Peter nails it later in 2:12 when he says, "Live such good lives among the pagans that, though they accuse you of doing wrong, they may see your good deeds and **glorify God** on the day He visits us."

And yes, "the day He visits us" refers (at least) to the Second Coming. But Jesus also visits us daily. He is risen! He lives now, this day within each believer, and is seen by those around us.

---

[71] Matthew 26:56b, 75b; Luke 22:62

Imagine what the Romans were thinking, as they watched these believers dying for their faith. "These (trials) have come so that your faith – of greater worth than gold, which perishes *even though refined by fire* - may be proved genuine . . ."

So here, Peter says, is the revelation.

Here is your purpose, revealed.

You're here on a mission to save a dying world. (Chosen, called, elect, holy) . . .

by revealing the nature of God . . .

by being Jesus (having His nature, His characteristics via the Holy Spirit).

And what are those characteristics?

Well, they all show up in the rest of the letter, but to continue to play the spoiler, let me share them now (and conveniently[72], they're alliterative!):

- Sacrificial
- Submissive
- Selfless
- Serving[73]
- Suffering[74]
- Self-denial
- Saved by grace
- Saving others

Interestingly, the characteristics of Satan are equally alliterative:

- Selfishness
- Satanic
- Self-preservation
- Separation from God and others

There is no doubt that the calling is difficult.

But Peter envisions the crown.

---

[72] . . . and because I was raised Baptist

[73] 4:10,11

[74] 1:6,11; 2:19,21; 3:14,17; 4:1,12-16,19; 5:1,9-10

He reinforces "the most important thing" when he reassures the recipients that they "are receiving the goal of your faith, **the salvation of your souls**." (I Peter 1:9, NIV) Yep, **it's the most important thing** to them; it's **the most important thing** to us; it's **the most important thing** to others.

⸮?⸮ QUESTIONS FOR REFLECTION

- Are you undergoing trials? Suffering? How does it compare with Peter's first century readers?
- Is your life your own? Who made you? Did you will yourself into existence?
- Would you have given your life to save your comrades, even if you were innocent?
- Are you autonomous? Captain of your own ship, master of your own fate? Doing things "your way?" How's that working out for you?

SIX

THE FOOLS

I Peter 1:8-12

". . . we defy augury[75]: there's a special providence in
the fall of a sparrow. If it be now, 'tis not to come;
if it be not to come, it will be now; if it be not now,
yet it will come: the readiness is all . . ."[76]

---

[75] augury: divination
[76] *Hamlet*, Act 5, Scene II (in response to Horatio's imploring Hamlet to back out
of his duel with Laertes), William Shakespeare

Polycarp, Bishop of Smyrna, was a disciple of the Apostle John, Peter's fishing partner. He was likely the last person alive who had seen and known an apostle. He was martyred for refusing to burn incense to Caesar. While not inspired, this is the account from eyewitnesses of the events surrounding his death:

"The police and horsemen came with the young man at suppertime on the Friday with their usual weapons, as if coming out against a robber. That evening, they found him lying down in the upper room of a cottage. He could have escaped but he refused saying, 'God's will be done.' When he heard that they had come, he went down and spoke with them. They were amazed at his age and steadfastness, and some of them said. 'Why did we go to so much trouble to capture a man like this?' Immediately he called for food and drink for them, and asked for an hour to pray uninterrupted. They agreed, and he stood and prayed, so full of the grace of God, that he could not stop for two hours. The men were astounded and many of them regretted coming to arrest such a Godly and venerable an old man.

When he finished praying, they put him on a donkey, and took him into the city.

As Polycarp was being taken into the arena, a voice came to him from heaven: 'Be strong, Polycarp and play the man!' No one saw who had spoken, but our brothers who were there heard the voice. When the crowd heard that Polycarp had been captured, there was an uproar. The Proconsul asked him whether he was Polycarp. On hearing that he was, he tried to persuade him to apostatize, saying, 'Have respect for your old age, swear by the fortune of Caesar. Repent, and say, 'Down with the Atheists!' Polycarp looked grimly at the wicked heathen multitude in the stadium, and gesturing towards them, he said, 'Down with the Atheists!'

'Swear,' urged the Proconsul, 'reproach Christ, and I will set you free.'

'Eighty and six years have I served Him,' Polycarp declared, 'and He has done me no wrong. How can I blaspheme my King and my Savior?'

'I have wild animals here,' the Proconsul said. 'I will throw you to them if you do not repent.'

'Call them,' Polycarp replied. 'It is unthinkable for me to repent from *what is good to turn to what is evil. I will be glad though to be changed from evil to righteousness.'*

'If you despise the animals, I will have you burned.'

'You threaten me with fire which burns for an hour, and is then extinguished, but you know nothing of the fire of the coming judgment and eternal punishment, reserved for the ungodly. Why are you waiting? Bring on whatever you want.'

It was all done in the time it takes to tell. The crowd collected wood and bundles of sticks from the shops and public baths. The Jews, as usual, were keen to help. When the pile was ready, Polycarp took off his outer clothes, undid his belt, and tried to take off his sandals – something he was not used to, as the faithful always raced to do it for him, each wanting to be the one to touch his skin – this is how good his life was. But when they went to fix him with nails, he said, 'Leave me as I am, for he that gives me strength to endure the fire, will enable me not to struggle, without the help of your nails.'

So, they simply bound him with his hands behind him like a distinguished ram chosen from a great flock for sacrifice. Ready to be an acceptable burnt-offering to God, he looked up to heaven, and said, 'O Lord God Almighty, the Father of your beloved and blessed Son Jesus Christ, by whom we have received the knowledge of You, the God of angels, powers and every creature, and of all the righteous who live before You, I give You thanks that You count me worthy to be numbered among your martyrs, sharing the cup of Christ and the resurrection to eternal life, both of soul and body, through the immortality of the Holy Spirit. May I be received this day as an acceptable sacrifice, as You, the true God, have predestined, revealed to me, and now fulfilled. I praise You for all these things, I bless You and glorify You, along with the everlasting Jesus Christ, your beloved Son. To You, with him, through the Holy Ghost, be glory both now and forever. Amen.'

Then the fire was lit, and the flame blazed furiously. We who were privileged to witness it saw a great miracle, and this is why we have been preserved, to tell the story. The fire shaped itself into the form of an arch, like the sail of a ship when filled with the wind, and formed a circle around the body of the martyr. Inside it, he looked not like flesh that is burnt, but like bread that is baked, or gold and silver glowing in a furnace. And we smelt a sweet scent, like frankincense or some such precious spices.

Eventually, when those wicked men saw that his body could not be consumed by the fire, they commanded an executioner to pierce him with a dagger."[77]

Peter saw Jesus. Literally and physically. Peter saw Jesus.

Peter saw Jesus' glory. In the miracles. At the Transfiguration. At the resurrection. At the ascension.

We didn't.

You and I haven't seen any of that. And neither had the recipients of this letter.

And yet, Peter does two things.

First, he applauds them. Perhaps he remembered his fellow disciple, Thomas, and his doubt of the resurrection. A doubt so strong, he swore he would not believe unless he could touch the wounds. Thomas had the opportunity to do just that. And then, he believed.[78]

You and I don't have that opportunity. And neither did our fellow believers in the first century. And Peter knows that.

> "Though you have not seen Him, you love Him; and even though you do not see Him now, you believe in Him and are filled with an inexpressible and glorious joy . . ." (I Peter 1:8, NIV)

And so, he reinforces to them how special and how valuable their faith is. This man, who had experienced all that he had experienced with Jesus, was urging them (us) to keep on believing, and that our belief is not in vain, and that our salvation is secure.

> ". . . for you are receiving the goal of your faith, the salvation of your souls." (I Peter 1:9, NIV)

Second, Peter reminds them of the prophets of old. Men and women who had gone before them, long since dead. They died without having seen Jesus as well.

---

[77] From a letter from eye-witnesses to other churches in the area, ca. 160 A.D.; Public Domain

[78] John 20:24-29

"Concerning this salvation, the prophets, who spoke of the grace that was to come to you, searched intently and with the greatest care, trying to find out the time and circumstances to which the Spirit of Christ in them was pointing when He predicted the sufferings of Christ and the glories that would follow." (I Peter 1:10-11, NIV)

They remained faithful to the death and never got to see the object of their faith.

Just.

Like.

Us.

I love how the Hebrew writer expresses it in the midst of the "Roll Call of the Faithful." That writer recounts the early patriarchs and their faith, then reminds the reader:

"All these people were still living by faith when they died. They did not receive the things promised; they only saw them and welcomed them from a distance."[79] (Hebrews 11:13a, NIV)

He then goes on to recount even more of the heroes of the faith. Then the writer comes back and reminds us a second time:

"These were all commended for their faith, yet none of them received what had been promised. God had planned something better for us so that only together with us would they be made perfect." (Hebrews 11:39-40, NIV)

What is so great about this passage is that Peter reminds us that we get to glimpse something others didn't. We get to know the physical reality of the Messiah, something the prophets never got to see. And yet, they remained faithful, even in the face of persecution, even in the face of death.

---

[79] Of note, the Hebrew writer goes on to say, "And they admitted that they were aliens and strangers on earth." (Hebrew 11:13b, NIV)

You and I can see that they were right in remaining faithful! We live on the other side of Jesus.

Because Peter has seen the resurrected Messiah, he can in turn assure and encourage us that our faith is not in vain. He can speak with the same authority to us as we can about those prophets. He has seen the other side of resurrection, just as we know the other side of the coming of the Messiah.

To their contemporaries, the prophets looked like fools. They looked ignorant. They lacked "common sense." And you have to ask the questions:

Why did they not fight?

Why did they not flee?

It's because ". . . things are not what they seem! God's [power] is the real power clothed in apparent powerlessness; Evil's [power] is apparent power which is really powerlessness."[80]

They understood **the most important thing**.

> "It was revealed to them that they were not serving themselves but you, when they spoke of the things that have now been told you by those who have preached the gospel to you by the Holy Spirit sent from heaven." (I Peter1:12a, NIV)

Michael Card is a gifted balladeer. God has used him powerfully to drive home this point. And in no greater way has He done so than through this song that changed my life:

God's Own Fool[81]
Seems I've imagined Him all of my life
As the wisest of all of mankind
But if God's Holy wisdom is foolish to men
He must have seemed out of His mind

For even His family said He was mad
And the priests said a demon's to blame

---

[80] Dr. Vernard Eller, 1927-2007
[81] Michael Card, 1989, by permission.

But God in the form of this angry young man
Could not have seemed perfectly sane

When we in our foolishness thought we were wise
He played the fool and He opened our eyes
When we in our weakness believed we were strong
He became helpless to show we were wrong
And so we follow God's own fool
For only the foolish can tell-
Believe the unbelievable
And come be a fool as well

So come lose your life for a carpenter's son
For a madman who died for a dream
And you'll have the faith His first followers had
And you'll feel the weight of the beam
So surrender the hunger to say you must know
Have the courage to say I believe
For the power of paradox opens your eyes
And blinds those who say they can see

So we follow God's own Fool
For only the foolish can tell
Believe the unbelievable,
And come be a fool as well

The prophets looked like fools for their behavior then . . . but were not.
We may look like fools for our behavior now . . . but are not.
(And if we don't look like fools for our behavior yet, maybe we will after we see where Peter is taking us. Keep going, dear Reader.)

??? QUESTIONS FOR REFLECTION

- Eyewitnesses recount that Polycarp could have escaped, but refused. Why? Would you have tried?
- Was Polycarp a fool?
- Were those members of the Roll Call of the Faithful fools?
- Where is God going?
- What's the most important thing?
- Who am I serving?
- If I am suffering, could it be that I am serving someone other than myself?
- If I'm not suffering, am I serving myself only?

SEVEN

THE PREP

I Peter 1:13-16

"God assumed from the beginning that the wise of the world
would view Christians as fools . . . and He has not been
disappointed. Be fools for Christ. And have the courage
to suffer the contempt of the sophisticated world."[82]

---

[82] Justice Antonin Scalia (1936-2016)

·· 7 ··

The oil boom of the early 1980s was in full tilt. Oklahoma oil fields were dotted with rigs thicker than trees, and small towns experienced the economic benefits along with the influx of folks looking to take advantage of the good times. Dr. Ronald Goodman[83] had been practicing medicine in his hometown for over fifteen years. With the good times, he welcomed a new associate, Dr. Michael Dane and his family into the practice.

Then came the bust.

People left. Money dried up. A decision had to be made. And it was.

Dr. Goodman gave up the practice he had built for the benefit of the new young family that he had welcomed into his town. He began teaching school with his wife at the local public school, with a substantial decrease in income. Dr. Dane was able to continue the practice alone.

You've heard the old salt before: "whenever you see the word 'therefore', you're about to find out what everything said before that is there . . . for!" In other words, what comes after "therefore" are generally action steps.

> "Therefore, prepare your minds for action; be self-controlled; set your hope fully on the grace to be given you when Jesus Christ is revealed. As obedient children, do not conform to the evil desires you had when you lived in ignorance. But just as He who called you is holy, so be holy in all you do; for it is written: 'Be holy, because I am holy.'" (I Peter 1:12-16)

Sure enough, this "therefore" is no exception. From this point in the first chapter until 5:11, Peter is going to tell and show us how to "set (our) hope fully on the grace to be given (us) when Jesus Christ is revealed." Because when he gets to the end at 5:12, Peter says, ". . . I have written to you briefly, encouraging you and testifying that **this is the true grace of God**. Stand fast in it." (I Peter 5:12b, NIV)

---

[83] Not his real name

Action Step #1: Prepare Your Minds

Peter begins this primer by admonishing us to "prepare (our) minds for action." We're right back to Paul's "renewing of our minds." But this is a battle call, because what this call entails does not come naturally. The next call itself screams unnatural: be self-controlled. What comes naturally is, instead, "flesh-controlled."

Action Step #2: Be Self-Controlled

In the circumstances that the recipients of this letter found themselves, the "flesh-controlled" response is evident: fight or flight. But Peter says, "Whoa! Tap the brakes. Control the body's impulse to fight. Stop the urge to flee." Exercise self-control. And the only way that this can happen is by the grace of Jesus. Set your hope on how you will look when you don't fight or flee. Jesus will be revealed! To anyone who sees your behavior. They will see the grace of Jesus on the cross manifested through you and your grace-filled behavior.

Action Step #3: Do Not Conform

But you have to prepare your mind for action. Peter tells us that we used to be ignorant, conforming to what came naturally, the "evil desires" that we had. But no more. Then here comes that descriptor of us: holy (set apart for a specific purpose).

Action Step #4: Be Holy

"Holiness starts in the mind."[84] [85]
Here's the contrast: evil desires versus holiness.
And here's the translation, the equation, if you will:

$$\text{evil desires} = \text{selfishness}$$
$$\text{holiness} = \text{selflessness.}$$

---

[84] Charles Swindoll, Senior Pastor, Stonebriar Community Church, Frisco, Texas
[85] For some more encouragement and insight, watch *Bob Newhart – Stop It*, YouTube

Peter's fellow apostle, Paul, initiates his list of what "terrible times in the last days" will look like with:

"People will be lovers of themselves . . ." (II Timothy 3:1-2a, NIV)

Frances Chan's take on this list is that "lover of self is the sewer pipe out of which all of the other garbage flows."

(Watch how this plays out.)

Peter then quotes multiple citations from Leviticus where God says, "Be holy, because I am holy"[86] (I Peter 1:16b, NIV) to remind us that this is exactly what our calling is: to be holy.

Oh, but Peter's just getting started.

---

[86] Leviticus 11:44,45; 19:2; 20:7 (NIV)

??? QUESTIONS FOR REFLECTION

- Was Dr. Goodman a fool? Did he not deserve to keep the practice he had built? Would you have given up your life's work to another?
- Whose example did he follow?[87]
- Are there any "evil desires" that are not selfish?
- Are there any sins that are not selfish?

---

[87] Genesis 13:1-12

EIGHT

THE CHOICE

I Peter 1:17-25

"I'd rather stand before Jesus and answer for giving
to a hundred people that didn't need it, than to
answer for turning down one that did."[88]

---

[88] Fred E. Mashburn, Jr. (1927-2012)

·· 8 ··

In the early portion of Les Misérables *by Victor Hugo, the convict Jean Valjean is released from a French prison after serving nineteen years for stealing a loaf of bread and for subsequent attempts to escape from prison. When Valjean arrives at the town of Digne, no one is willing to give him shelter because he is an ex-convict. Desperate, a disheveled Valjean knocks on the door of Monseigneur Myriel, the kindly bishop of Digne. Ignoring the repeated warnings of his housekeeper that Valjean is a monster who will kill them, Myriel treats Valjean with kindness, feeding him and giving him a bed to sleep in. Valjean repays the bishop by stealing his silverware.*

When the police arrest Valjean, the bishop covers for him, claiming that the silverware was a gift. The authorities release Valjean and Myriel makes him promise to become an honest man, with the admonishment that "there is more rejoicing in heaven over the face of a repentant sinner than the white, silk robes of a hundred just men."

Is this the day I die?
Yep.
We were fooled.
And we were fools.
It's a fact:

We.

Will.

Die.

In fact, at some time in the future, everything we know, everything we see, will be gone. It will all perish. Or it will be changed.

Peter knew this. And it sounds pretty depressing. Unless you know the whole story. Unless you see the big picture. Because all that we are able to sense will, in fact, be gone. But there are some things that are eternal. And aren't those the things that matter? God thinks so. Peter thinks so. Then maybe so should we. And so, Peter contrasts perishable things with imperishable things.

> "For you know that it was not with perishable things such as silver or gold that you were redeemed from the empty way of life handed down to you from your forefathers . . ." (I Peter 1:18, NIV)

> "For you have been born again, not of perishable seed . . ." (I Peter 1:23a, NIV)

> "For, 'all men are like grass, and all their glory is like the flowers of the field; the grass withers and the flowers fall . . .'" (I Peter 1:24, NIV)

So, what goes?
The "perishable":

- silver,
- gold,
- "empty way of life",
- perishable seed,
- men,
- grass,
- flowers.

And what stays?

> ". . . but [you were redeemed] with the precious blood of Christ, a lamb without blemish or defect." (I Peter 1:18, 19, NIV)

"... [you have been born again] ... through the living and enduring word of God." (I Peter 1:23, NIV)

"... but the word of the Lord stands forever." (I Peter 1: 25, NIV)

What stays is the "imperishable":

- blood of Christ,
- lamb without blemish,
- imperishable seed,
- Word of God,
- Word of the Lord.

Remember that Peter had witnessed the Rich Young Ruler.[89] He had heard Jesus contrast the perishable and the imperishable. He had seen the young man's face fall. Peter had to remember the amazement that he and the other disciples felt as they saw Jesus let the young man walk away. And perhaps Peter even chuckled a little now, now that he got it ... now that he understood the calling ... now that he knew **the most important thing**.

So, a hundred years from now, when we're all forgotten, what will we have hitched our wagon to?

Or perhaps a more important question would be what are we hitching our wagon to today? And how does it impact our mission? The "empty way of life handed down to (us) from our forefathers" was all about self:

- Self survival
- Self fulfillment
- Self assurance
- Self esteem
- Self governing
- Self satisfaction

But none of that bought us what we wanted. We could only be bought, we could only be redeemed with something selfless: the blood of One who

---

[89] Mark 10:17-31

sacrificed Self wholly for us. And hitching our wagon to Jesus ensures that *His* mission becomes *our* mission.

The opening verse and chorus of the old Crosby hymn[90] say it better than any prose:

> Redeemed, how I love to proclaim it!
> Redeemed by the blood of the Lamb;
> Redeemed through His infinite mercy,
> His child and forever I am.
>
> Refrain:
> Redeemed, redeemed,
> Redeemed by the blood of the Lamb;
> Redeemed, redeemed,
> His child and forever I am.

Who has the right to tell you what to do? Who has the right to be your "king?" Only Jesus paid the ultimate price for you and for me. Is there any other who merits our obedience? Is there anything that is worthy of our allegiance? Only Jesus has the right to call us to obedience.

---

[90] "Redeemed, How I Love to Proclaim It!", 1882, Fanny Crosby, (1820-1915)

??? QUESTIONS FOR REFLECTION

- Have you given any thought to your mortality?
- Can you remember anything about any of your great grandparents? What about great, great grandparents? Do you even know anything about them?
- Was Monseigneur Myriel a fool for treating Jean Valjean with kindness? Did he endanger his life and the life of his housekeeper? Was he a fool for covering for Valjean? Did the Bishop have any assurance of Valjean's subsequent use of the funds from the silver?
- Have you ever given of yourself (time, money, goods) suspecting that what you gave would be wasted?
- Who is responsible to God? The giver? The receiver? Both?
- Who is the judge?

NINE

THE LOVE

I Peter 1:22, 2:1-3

"What is the good of words if they aren't important enough
to quarrel over? Why do we choose one word more than another
if there isn't any difference between them? If you called
a woman a chimpanzee instead of an angel, wouldn't there
be a quarrel about a word? If you're not going to argue
about words, what are you going to argue about? Are you
going to convey your meaning to me by moving your ears? The
Church and the heresies always used to fight about words,
because they are the only thing worth fighting about."[91]

---

[91] G. K. Chesterton (1874-1936)

Anyone who's been around me for very long soon learns that I'm a Beatles fan. A child of the sixties (1960s!), I still remember[92] the first time I ever heard anyone say the name. It was 1964. I was in Mrs. Prater's fifth grade classroom at Washington Irving Elementary. And it was from a classmate who said in a rather disparaging manner, "Haven't you heard of the Beatles?" And I still remember listening to their first U.S. hit, *I Want to Hold Your Hand*, on the only radio in the house, a rather large brown box with Zenith on the front of it sitting in the kitchen. And I can still well remember my thirty-year-old mother commenting as she did the dishes, "I don't know how anyone can listen to all that noise."

For those who didn't grow up in the sixties, it is impossible to explain the impact that four lads from Liverpool, England had on the world. The influence they had on the Boomer generation would be hard to measure. But one significant area that indelibly bore their stamp was that of "love." And the world has never been the same.

I Want to Hold Your Hand was replaced after seven weeks at number one on Billboard's chart with *She Loves You*. And that was the first of an even dozen Beatles tunes with the word "love" in the title (not to mention the countless others with love as a theme).

While they were not the only rockers to carry the "free love" banner (with all of its combinations and permutations), they were certainly the most popular and most visible. All they needed was the Pill and a little help from Dr. Spock's[93] permissive raising of the Boomers, and "love was all around."[94]

In 1967, the Beatles released *All You Need Is Love*. Written by John Lennon and Paul McCartney, the song became an anthem. When asked in 1971 whether songs like *Give Peace a Chance* and *Power to the People* were propaganda songs, Lennon answered: "Sure. So was *All You Need Is Love*. I'm a revolutionary artist. My art is dedicated to change." And while some

---

[92] With all due respect to my Brother, David MacSmith, who constantly reminds me that "if you remember the sixties, you really weren't there."

[93] *Baby and Child Care*, Dr. Benjamin Spock, 1946 – Dr. Spock's book was a mainstay in the libraries of most of the parents of the Boomers.

[94] The Troggs, "Love Is All Around", 1967

might argue over the message and propaganda and influence associated with *Give Peace a Chance* and *Power to the People*, who could argue with *All You Need Is Love*? As the Beatles manager, Brian Epstein said, "The nice thing about it is that it cannot be misinterpreted. It is a clear message saying that love is everything."

Right.

That summer, 1967, became known as "The Summer of Love", and an entire movement sprang up around the word. Seems innocent enough. After all, God is love, (I John 4:16b, NIV) right?

Here's the rub. What does "love" mean?

"We're using the same vocabulary, but a different dictionary."[95]

I mean, we love our puppies, we love our grandmother, we love apple pie, and we love America. We love to dance and we love to run. We love the Beatles and we love our spouse. We love home. We love our job. We love the rain and we love the sun. And "Jesus loves me, this I know, for the Bible tells me so."[96]

Is all that love the same?

Of course not.

The problem with the word is a problem with our language. In English, we only have the one word to describe multiple feelings and actions. And that word is translated from the Greek into Scripture in our only word: love.

So why in the world did I take all of this time and ink to stroll down memory lane, and what does all of this have to do with Peter . . . or Rome . . . or me?

Stay with me. Listen to Peter:

> "Now that you have purified yourselves by obeying the truth so that you have sincere love for your brothers, love one another deeply from the heart." (I Peter 1:22, NIV)

The Greek language has four words that get translated to the English word "love", and they all four have very different connotations,

---

[95] John Stonestreet, President, Colson Center for Christian Worldview

[96] Lyrics (1860), Anna Bartlett Warner (1827-1915); Music (1862), William Bradbury (1816-1868)

applications, and implications. Each has different demands, different levels of commitment and emotion. And they are not interchangeable. And understanding First Peter hinges in part on our understanding of love.

So, let's take a few minutes to explore the four loves of Greek.

Storgeo

- "natural love"
- (think "family love" e.g. parent/child)
- not found in the New Testament (except in compound: *astorgos*)

Phileo

- "brotherly love"
- (think "Phila-delphia," the "city of brotherly love")
- highly subjective and based on the loveliness or attractiveness *of an object*

Erao

- "passionate love"
- (think "erotic" . . . it is the derivative word for our English word)
- strong desires ranging from patriotic to sexual love
- popularized in western culture in everything from *That's Amore*[97] to *Hello, I Love You (Won't You Tell Me Your Name)*[98]

Agapao

- "God-love"
- (think "Jesus" . . . though mankind deserved nothing but rejection and wrath, God sacrificed His one and only Son for man's salvation. Between God and sinful man, there was no *phileo* to speak of. This was done for man's good and solely because God, the subject, accorded him this wholly underserved value.)

---

[97] Dean Martin, 1953
[98] The Doors, 1968

- action which is done for the benefit of that object being loved
- rooted in the mind and will of the subject and means to value, esteem, prize, treat as precious; to be devoted to
- *agapao* is done by the lover for the beloved **even if it costs the lover**

Now do you see why it's so difficult for us to talk about "love" in English?

But next comes a very important distinction between the four loves. In fact, recognizing this distinction is critical to understanding what Peter wants us to get when he speaks of love in this letter.

As you can see from the explanations above, there is a varying degree of emotion involved in each of the loves described. Let's try to take them one at a time.

First, *storgeo*, family love. On the scale below, most of us would put *storgeo* fairly far toward the right of the scale. Most of us have strong emotions toward our family, lots of "warm fuzzies."

Next, *phileo*, brotherly love. Again, this type of love elicits fairly strong emotions, so it, too, tilts toward the right side of the scale. We feel warmth and kinship to those who support the same things, whether it's a football team or a community.

Third, *erao*, erotic love. Put this one all the way to the right. Nothing trumps this one for emotion. In most cases, the will and the mind are thrown out in favor of the feeling. It rings the bell on the emotion end of the scale.

Last, *agapao*, God love. Yep, this one goes all the way to the left. It is "to will the good of the other."[99] The bullet points listed on the previous page pretty well summarize this love. It is a love that acts with no regard to (and sometimes in spite of) the feeling or emotion. It does what is in the best interest of the one being loved regardless of the cost to the one doing the loving. Think Jesus on the cross.

DECISION OF
THE WILL   EMOTION

I---I

Agapao   *Phileo Storgeo Erao*

---

[99] St. Thomas Aquinus (1225-1274)

And it's with that background that Peter encourages the recipients (and us) to move from the *phileo* that they have, to the *agapao* that God calls us to. We could even add those words to our earlier list of perishable and imperishable. After all, Peter places them right in the middle of his contrasts. The *phileo* will perish, but *agapao* (God-love) will not perish.

What is Peter trying to get them/us to do? He's telling us that selfless acts are the acts we are called to perform as our mission. He's saying that we need to decide to do what is in the best interest of the person in front of us . . . regardless of the cost to us. Peter is indeed covering the Beatles, saying, "All you need is love", but what he's really saying is, "All you need is *agapao*."

And how do I do this, Peter? How do I move from the perishable to the imperishable? How do I *agapao*?

"I'm glad you asked that question."

"Therefore, rid yourselves of all malice and all deceit, hypocrisy, envy, and slander of every kind. Like newborn babies, crave pure spiritual milk, so that by it you may grow up in your salvation, now that you have tasted that the Lord is good." (I Peter 2:1-3, NIV)

It's just a matter of moving from the immature (selfish) to the mature (selfless). Feed the part of you that will last. He could very well have taken a lesson from his fellow apostle, Paul's playbook from the thirteenth chapter of First Corinthians.

> ". . . when perfection (maturity) comes, the imperfect (immature) disappears. When I was a child, I talked like a child, I thought like a child, I reasoned like a child. When I became a man, I put childish ways behind me." (I Corinthians 13:10-11, NIV)

Quit being a baby and grow up.

??? QUESTIONS FOR REFLECTION

- Which brothers are they / am I to *agape*? (See 1:22) The nice ones? The kind ones? The ones that treat us like we oughta be treated?
- What about . . . the deceivers? The hypocrites? The envious? The slanderers?
- Why should they (or why should I) *agapao* even the imperfect, the sinners? Do they/I have any other kind of brothers?

TEN

THE ROCK

First Peter 2:4-8

"Choosing to suffer means that there must be something
wrong with you, but choosing God's will - even if it means
you will suffer - is something very different. No normal,
healthy saint ever chooses suffering; he simply chooses God's
will just as Jesus did, whether it means suffering or not.
And no saint should ever dare to interfere with the lesson
of suffering being taught in another saint's life."[100]

---

[100] Oswald Chambers, *My Utmost for His Highest*, August 16

In the Christmas classic It's a Wonderful Life[101], *young George Bailey (played by Jimmy Stewart) dreams of "shakin' the dust off" his little hometown of Bedford Falls to "see the world." But in one crisis after another, George is forced to choose between sacrificing <u>his</u> dreams for the needs of others. And he always sacrifices. Then, faced with the fact that not only will he never realize his dreams, but instead facing impending personal and financial ruin, George contemplates ending his life. Saved by Clarence Odbody, his guardian angel, George nonetheless despairs that "it would have been better if I'd never been born at all."*

So, Clarence arranges it.

"You've been given a great gift, George," Clarence explains. "A chance to see what the world would be like without you." And what a different world it is.

George's idyllic hometown of Bedford Falls becomes Pottersville. A town that is dark and full of sin and corruption. A town whose inhabitants live in rented shacks instead of owning the nice homes that George's Building and Loan had helped them to buy. His selfless friends have become selfish. His Uncle Billy is institutionalized when the Building and Loan fails because George is not there to manage it. Mr. Gower, a pharmacist saved by George from accidentally poisoning a patient, is a drunk, just released from prison for manslaughter. Mary, George's wife, introverts in his absence and never marries.

And in the climactic scene, in a cemetery where the homes George helped to build would have been, George instead sees his brother Harry's grave; Clarence explains that not only did his brother die, but scores of soldiers aboard a transport ship during World War II died because Harry was not there to save them, since George was not around to save Harry from drowning at age nine.

"You see, George," says Clarence, "you really had a wonderful life. Don't you see what a mistake it would be to throw it away?"

---

[101] It's no secret that my favorite movie is "It's a Wonderful Life." I have it on VHS and DVD . . . in black and white, and colorized . . . original and digitally remastered. For our fortieth anniversary, Pam gave me a watch with "It's a Wonderful Life" engraved on the back. We named our cabin at Beaver's Bend State Park "It's a Wonderful Life Retreat" complete with posters from the movie in the game room.

And George does see. He begs God to let him live, even if it means facing scandal and arrest. I won't spoil the end for those who haven't made it through the movie. Let me just say that, even after dozens and dozens of screenings, I still get choked up when Harry toasts his brother as "the richest man in town."

You see, George Bailey didn't see the whole story. He didn't see that he was part of something much bigger than himself, that in selfless act after selfless act, George Bailey (as my mentor would so eloquently put it) "never let the good things in life rob him of the best."

Peter finishes out the second section on our calling by figuratively cementing us to our Cornerstone and to each other. His binding of us to Jesus becomes critical when we discover what its implications are. And his binding of us to each other serves to give us the encouragement we must have to behave in the manner to which we're about to be called . . . because it's gonna be a tough calling!

"As you come to Him, the living Stone – rejected by men but chosen by God and precious to Him – you also, like living stones, are being built into a spiritual house to be a holy priesthood, offering spiritual sacrifices acceptable to God through Jesus Christ. For in Scripture it says:

'See, I lay a Stone in Zion,
A chosen and precious cornerstone,
And the one who trusts in Him
will never be put to shame.'

Now to you who believe, this Stone is precious. But to those who do not believe,

'The Stone the builders rejected
Has become the Capstone,'

and,

'A Stone that causes men to stumble
And a Rock that makes them fall.'

They stumble because they disobey the message – which is also what they were destined for." (I Peter 2:4-8, NIV)

Do you think that it's coincidence that Peter takes this whole section of his letter to talk about stones?

After all, this was the man who had his name changed to "Rocky" (Gr. *petros*) by the Master. This was the man who had his confession declared the rock (Gr. *petra*) on which Jesus would build His church. And all of this occurred at Caesarea Philippi, a city of rocky cliffs with pagan shrines carved within the rock walls of those cliffs.

No, no, Rocky knows rocks. And I think Peter knew exactly what he was doing.

He uses the analogy of stones in a "spiritual house" to draw a picture for his readers of a structure of which each of us is a part. Alone, we're just a pebble. And without Jesus, "the Cornerstone", we're just a pile of rocks. But together, we have structure, we have meaning, and we tell a story.

It's the difference between Cougar Mountain and Mt. Rushmore.[102] It's the difference between Pottersville and Bedford Falls.

And in order to bear up under the weight of this calling . . .

We. Will. Need. Each other.

And . . . We. Will. Need. Jesus . . . because without Jesus, we'll crumble.

Peter has already, and will continue to point to Jesus, to "make a beeline to the cross." He hammers home our need to constantly be reminded of how Jesus was treated . . . and how Jesus behaved. We will not only need each other.

We. Will. Need. Jesus.

Three times, Peter refers to Jesus' rejection.[103] He's continuing to prepare us for the calling: rejection, hostility, persecution, suffering. Jesus was rejected. We will be rejected. Men were hostile toward Jesus. Men will be hostile toward us. Jesus played the fool for us. We will be asked to play the fool for others.

---

[102] Cougar Mountain was one of many names for the granite cliffs in South Dakota that were carved into what we now know and revere as Mt. Rushmore.
[103] Vss. 4,7,8

But the contrast is between the hostility of unbelieving men toward Jesus, and God's exaltation of Him.

God chose Jesus as precious and we know the outcome. We, also, are precious in God's sight and can be assured of the outcome, regardless of how we may be treated. Knowing the outcome, knowing the endgame, gives us the assurance, the motivation to act, to behave as Jesus.

Unbelieving men were hostile to Jesus.

God exalted Jesus.

Unbelieving men will be hostile to you (us).

God will exalt you.

And that segues perfectly into the final thought of Section Two.

¿?¿ QUESTION FOR REFLECTION

- Do I have to know the outcome of my situation to decide how to behave?

ELEVEN

THE MERCY

First Peter 2:9-12

"Loyalty to God is more important than life itself. The world's highest goal is to preserve physical life, but that is not the highest goal of your life, Christian. Our highest goal is to obey God, even if that means losing our physical life."[104]

---

[104] Dr. David Platt, Pastor, McLean Bible Church; Author; Former President of the Southern Baptist Convention International Mission Board

Tommy Pigage was the kind of kid most people would love to hate.

Two days before Christmas in 1982, twenty-four-year-old Tommy met eighteen-year-old Ted Morris on the Canton Street Bridge in Hopkinsville, Kentucky. Tommy was in a Buick; Ted was in an AMC Hornet. The meeting was head-on. The Hornet lost . . . and so did Ted. Tommy walked away with a blood alcohol level three times the legal limit; Ted was carried away and died four hours after the accident.

And the comparisons don't stop there.

Tommy had a part-time job in a music store. Ted was a scholarship student at David Lipscomb. Tommy was shy and directionless. Ted was outgoing and deeply committed to Jesus. Tommy was from a broken family and an alcoholic. Ted was the only son of loving parents, Frank and Elizabeth.

And those parents were bitter about their loss.

Originally charged with murder, Tommy pled not guilty. A Grand Jury reduced his charge to second-degree manslaughter, and he eventually was given a ten-year sentence. Five years were suspended and the other five were probated. Tommy Pigage was released.

And through each successive hearing, the bitterness and loathing of the Morrises grew towards Tommy. He was free. Ted was dead.

But one of the stipulations of Tommy's probation included speaking before students for Mothers Against Drunk Driving (MADD). And Tommy's first speech was at Trigg County High School, Ted's alma mater.

A leader of MADD, Elizabeth Morris was there.

After hearing Tommy accept responsibility for his actions, Elizabeth changed. Her bitterness turned into compassion . . . and she forgave.

But Elizabeth and Frank did more.

After violating the terms of his parole, Tommy was incarcerated. His most frequent visitor was Elizabeth Morris. Eventually, Judge Edwin White ordered Tommy released to the Morris's custody for church and other outings. He continued to lecture for MADD. And on the way from a MADD lecture in Todd County, Kentucky, on January 12, 1985, Frank Morris baptized the man who had killed his son into Christ at the Little River Church of Christ.

Tommy Pigage, the young man who had robbed them of their only son was now a brother in Christ to Frank and Elizabeth Morris. Both had forgiven

Tommy. But they went further. The Morrises all but "adopted" Tommy. They brought him into their home and have treated him as they would their own son. They talk by phone daily. They study the Bible and enjoy their time together.

Elizabeth told People *magazine, "because we've tried to help Tommy doesn't mean we love Ted any less. Ted has gone to a better place. If he knew about this hatred I was harboring toward Tommy, he would have said to forgive. Ted would not have wanted me hating Tommy, that hatred eating me like a cancer from inside. Now I can be happy again, I can go on living."[105]*

> "But you are a chosen people, a royal priesthood, a holy nation, a people belonging to God, that you may declare the praises of Him who called you out of darkness into His wonderful light. Once you were not a people, but now you are the people of God;" (I Peter 2:9-10a, NIV)

If it seems like Peter is trying to wear us out with constant reminders of who we are, keep in mind that he has a purpose. We are strangers in a strange land. And our task is daunting. Peter is much as the coach of a heavily underdogged team. He sits in "Babylon" (Jewish code for the seat of evil). He knows the encouragement his "team" will need in the days to come.

And Peter once again reminds his team (which includes us) that our behavior will show Jesus to the lost and dying world around us. Our purpose is to "declare the praises of Him who called you." (I Peter 2:9b, NIV)

But in the midst of his reminder, Peter invokes mercy.

> ". . . once you had not received mercy, but now you have received mercy." (I Peter 2:10b, NIV)

And since he talks of mercy in the midst of "testifying . . . the true grace of God" (I Peter 5:12, NIV), this is a good time to make a contrast, the contrast between grace and mercy. As we go forward into Section

---

[105] William Plummer, *People* Magazine, August 26, 1985

Three, and as we face a more challenging calling, understanding the meaning of the two words becomes important.

So, let's look:

MERCY (Gr. "eleos")

- (think "the good Samaritan" from Luke 10:30-35)
- often inadequately defined merely as clemency or forgiveness, holding back deserved punishment or affliction . . .
- more completely: the expression of pity, the action taken out of compassion for others in which one undertakes to alleviate their misery and relieve their suffering

GRACE (Gr. "charis")

- (think "Acts 2:38")
- especially used to describe favors done without expectation of return . . . unearned and unmerited favor
- it may express itself in the form of gifts or endowments (e.g. the Holy Spirit in the case of God), but they do not constitute grace in the proper sense

Let me see if I can contrast the two terms a little bit more in this way.

Think of "normalcy". In this case, normalcy refers to a relationship. Could be husband and wife; could be brother and sister; could be friend to friend. Sin comes in to disrupt the normalcy. It could be anything from a lie, to an infidelity, to physical harm. Whatever the case, however mild or severe the disruption, enmity has formed in the relationship. In order to restore normalcy to the relationship, something has to give. One party or the other has to make a move.

In the case of mercy, the offended party chooses not to mete out the punishment appropriate to the offense. They choose to not bestow on the offender that which the defender rightly deserves. Normalcy theoretically is restored.

But in the case of grace, not only is mercy extended and normalcy restored, but the offended goes beyond normalcy and bestows on the offender something that the offender never expected and certainly didn't deserve . . . a gift.

Almost all of the stories recounted in this book exemplify grace, often beyond belief. Think Frank & Elizabeth Morris.t

And nobody understood grace better than Peter.

He received it when Jesus restored him three times[106] for his thrice denial of his Savior[107]. Jesus not only forgave him and restored the relationship to its normalcy; he gave Peter charge over his "lambs" and "sheep." Jesus gave Peter the gift of confidence.

Peter then preached God's grace on those gathered on the Day of Pentecost. And in one of my favorite passages[108], Peter plays Monty Hall.[109] When the Jews were convicted that they had indeed crucified the Messiah ("cut to the heart"), they asked Peter, "Brothers, what shall we do?"

Imagine their remorse. They now understood that the One that had been prophesied, the One that their parents, and grandparents, and ancestors had looked forward to, the One who would deliver them, had been crucified . . . and that they were complicit in His murder. In fact, some of the same people in this audience were no doubt in the audience seven weeks earlier shouting, "Crucify Him! Crucify Him!" and were guilty of having delivered Him to the Romans to be executed.

They blew it! And they knew it!

Can you imagine the anguish in their voices when they cried, "Brothers, what shall we do?!"

And can you imagine Peter, perhaps remembering Jesus' restoration of him and Jesus' extension of grace to him, replying, "Repent and be baptized, every one of you, in the name of Jesus Christ (Messiah) for the forgiveness of your sins. And you will receive the gift of the Holy Spirit. The promise is for you and your children and for all who are far off – for all whom the Lord our God will call."

---

[106] John 21:15-19

[107] John 18:15-18, 25-26

[108] Acts 2:38-39

[109] For those unfamiliar with Monty Hall, he was the original host of the TV game show, Let's Make a Deal. The culmination of the show was "The Big Deal", where contestants would select from three doors onstage. One held a "zonk" (LMAD code for something worthless), the second held a modest prize, and the third held a very valuable prize, often a car.

OK. So, Monty Hall?

Yeah, here's where Monty (and grace) come in.

They (and by extension, we) had killed God. They had executed the Messiah. They had not only wrongly crucified a man, they had rid the earth of the very One sent to save them.

They deserved to die.

Peter (Monty) first of all gives them what's behind Door Number One: mercy. He tells them to be baptized in Jesus' name and they will be forgiven of having killed Him.

Normalcy restored.

But then, they not only get what's behind Door Number One, they also get what's behind Door Number Two: grace. Peter tells them that they will receive the *gift* of the Holy Spirit!

Can you see the jaws dropping?

But Peter's not finished.

The tears of joy have hardly begun when Mom realizes that Dad's not there . . . or the kids. Mary realizes that her sister, Dinah didn't make it to the temple today. And Baruch remembers his cousin, Chaim, who lives in Galilee.

No problem, says Peter. This gift, this grace goes beyond this place and this time. You also get what's behind Door Number Three. Because this promise is for not only you, but your children and for all who are far off. (Hey, that's you and me! "Far off" in both time and space.)

Yeah, Peter understood grace and mercy. He had not only received grace, but Peter got to be God's agent to extend grace to those gathered in Jerusalem on that Day of Pentecost. And by extension, he extended it to us, for we are as guilty as they. We would have done the same thing then. We do the same thing now when we sin.

Then Peter closes out our Section Two reminding us to . . .

> "Live such good lives among the pagans that, though they accuse you of doing wrong, they may see your good deeds and glorify God on the day He visits us." (I Peter 2:12, NIV)

. . . the day He visits us . . .

The Day of Judgement? Sure. But also, doesn't He visit us when He comes to live in a repentant sinner's heart? And wouldn't He be glorified in their salvation and subsequent life? And remember, after all . . .

What's **the most important thing**?!?

That is our mission. We're aliens and strangers in the world, a world captive to the evil one. As Twila Paris puts it in *Rescue the Prisoner*[110]

> But this is not the enemy
> Flesh and blood have been deceived
> When we move beyond the anger
> We will see
>
> We've got to rescue the prisoner
> Rescue the prisoner
> Prisoner of war
> That's what He came here for

Frank and Elizabeth Morris understood . . . and they rescued one more prisoner from the enemy.

OK, my friend. We waded through the why, the purpose of life. Now it's time to dive off into the how. In light of the why, how do we live in the real world? You've stayed with me so far. Now the going gets tough, so let's look together and see what God has for us to discover in the next section.

---

[110] Twila Paris, 1993

??? QUESTIONS FOR REFLECTION

- Has God extended mercy to me? How? When?
- Has God extended grace to me? How? When?
- Is there a situation in which God would not extend grace and mercy to me? Is there a sin so egregious that He would not extend grace and mercy to me?
- Could you have extended mercy to Tommy Pigage if he had killed your only son? Even when he continued to drink?
- Could you have extended true grace to Tommy Pigage?
- Will Tommy Pigage and Ted Morris see each other in heaven? Who did God use to bring that meeting about?
- Is there a situation in which I should not extend grace and mercy to another? Is there a sin so egregious that I could not extend grace or mercy?
- How do I "declare the praises of Him who called you out of darkness into His wonderful light?" (2:9)
- What "good deeds" will the pagans see? (2:12) Is *People* magazine (where a lengthy account of Tommy and the Morris family appeared) a "Christian" magazine? How many non-Christians do you suppose read this account? How did Frank and Elizabeth Morris declare the praises of Jesus?

SECTION THREE

Preacher John always extolled the value of "man's best friend", the dog. He noted that they were wonderful companions for the elderly, and that they served well as seeing-eye dogs, for example. Every Sunday he had some heartwarming story about one of the parishioner's dogs.

One day he decided to put a cement sidewalk along the church's city block. He built the frame, mixed the concrete, poured it, and proudly smoothed the surface. It was a magnificent job. No sooner had he finished than a neighbor's dog came running along and trotted straight down the center of the wet cement. Preacher John went back and smoothed out the footprints and completely repaired the damaged sidewalk. The dog immediately returned and danced around in the wet sidewalk again. Preacher John again repaired the damage. This did not deter the dog; he came back and again traipsed through the fine work for a third time. This time the preacher went into his house and got his shotgun and shot the dog right on the spot.

The next day one of the parishioners was very puzzled and asked the preacher how he could have shot the dog; didn't he always say that dogs did a wonderful service for people? John answered, "Yes, I love dogs in the abstract, but not in the concrete."

OK. It's a lame joke, but it's one of my preaching minister's[111] favorites. And it serves to prepare us for what Peter is about to say to us. Up to this point, Peter has talked in abstracts and generalizations.

No more.

Now, Peter "gets in our business", in the concrete. He challenges the reader to live out the life of Jesus, to "deny himself and take up his cross and follow Me"[112], to quote the Savior. So, hold on. Put aside your preconceived ideas about what "denying yourself" or "taking up your cross" means, and hold on. This could be a bumpy ride.

---

[111] Todd Catteau
[112] Matthew 16:24, Matthew 10:38, Luke 9:23, Luke 14:27 (NIV)

TWELVE

THE CITIZEN

First Peter 2:13-17

"Submit yourselves for the Lord's sake to every authority
instituted among men: whether to the king . . ."
(I Peter 2:13, NIV)

·· 12 ··

OK. Stop right there.

Who's the king?

Caesar. Probably Nero. Remember, we've already set the stage for this in Chapter Two. This guy is out of his mind. He's killing Christians, possibly within earshot of Peter. Possibly within a short enough distance for Peter to smell the flesh of his burning brothers and sisters or hear their cries. Traditionally, the killing eventually reaches Peter's doorstep.

Surely Peter couldn't mean *this* king. He means only the good ones, right?

"Submit yourselves for the Lord's sake to every authority instituted among men: whether to the king, as the supreme authority, or to governors, who are sent by him to punish those who do wrong and to commend those who do right." (I Peter 2:13-14, NIV)

No qualifiers, huh, Peter?

Besides, he goes on to say that these authorities' responsibility is to "punish those who do wrong and to commend those who do right." So, all we have to do is do what's right and we'll be OK, right? That will "silence the talk of foolish men" (I Peter 2:15, NIV) and Nero will leave us alone, right?

And if he doesn't, then we're justified in not submitting to him, correct?

Well, not exactly.

Peter doubles down in the last verse in the paragraph when he tells the reader to "Show proper respect to everyone: Love the brotherhood of believers, fear God, **honor the king**." (I Peter 2:17, NIV)

Which kings does Peter say to submit to?

Which kings does Peter say to respect?

Which kings does Peter say to honor?

The good ones? The bad ones?

Peter had a perfectly good opportunity here to qualify his admonition . . . and he didn't take it. Not only that, he tells us that it is God's will to do good[113] . . . regardless of the consequences. And not just regardless of the consequences, but in order to accomplish something: the mission. Remember . . .

---

[113] I Peter 2:15 (NIV)

What's **the most important thing**?

David knew. And David knew about honoring dishonorable kings. Saul was king. Israel's king. David's king.

David had served in King Saul's service. He had been in Saul's court and given him relief from an evil spirit through the playing of his harp. David had saved the honor of Saul and the Israelites by defeating Goliath and the Philistines. He served as Saul's general and defeated Israel's enemies for his King time after time. David even became Saul's son-in-law.

Yet the King was jealous of David, and "remained his enemy the rest of his days." (II Kings 18:29, NIV) Even to the point of seeking David's death. On multiple occasions, Saul put David in harm's way in battle for no other reason than to have David die in battle. Yet the more Saul tried to have David killed, the more God granted David success against the enemy in battle.

Saul tried to pin David to the wall with his spear even as David was ministering to his King with his music. He sent men to David's house to kill him, then to pursue him when he escaped.

Finally, King Saul himself pursued David.

And on two occasions, as Saul sought David's life, David had the opportunity to kill Saul. On both occasions, David's men encouraged him to kill Saul, even invoking God's blessing: "This is the day the Lord spoke of when He said to you, 'I will give your enemy into your hands for you to deal with as you wish.'" (I Samuel 24:4, NIV) And even a second time: "Today God has delivered your enemy into your hands." (I Samuel 26:8, NIV)

David's response?

"The Lord forbid that I should do such a thing to my master, the Lord's anointed, or lift my hand against him; for he is the anointed of the Lord." (I Samuel 24:6, NIV)

"Don't destroy him! Who can lay a hand on the Lord's anointed and be guiltless? As surely as the Lord lives, the Lord Himself will strike him; either his time will come and he will die, or he will go into battle and perish. But the Lord forbid that I should lay a hand on the Lord's anointed." (I Samuel 26:9-11a, NIV)

Tommy Nelson gives us some great Biblical principles for dealing with conflict.[114] Here are the first three:

1. **Don't react.** Tommy emphasizes the etymological power of the word "react" in this case. It means don't re-enact what the offender did to you. When we're wronged, we believe we're bound by the principle of justice to act as judge[115], jury, and executioner. We find the offender guilty and judge them worthy of punishment, i.e. they deserve to get the same offense as we did. Ah, but then there's the issue of punitive (for punishment) damages; damages that are inflicted on the offender to deter them from doing it again.

   So, here's the picture: you hit me on the arm; I hit you on the cheek. You cheat once on me; I cheat twice on you. You tell a lie to me; I tell a worse lie to you. But you see what happens? It only escalates from there, and there is no end to the mischief that ensues. (As Tommy puts it, "She throws the cushion; he throws the chair!")

2. **Respond to God.** Jesus is our standard of behavior, not the other person. The offender does not set the standard; God does. This is what Peter says when he encourages the reader to "live as free men, but do not use your freedom as a cover-up for evil; live as servants of God." (I Peter 2:16, NIV)

3. **Let God change 'em.** It is the Holy Spirit's job to change the offender, not the responsibility of the offended. Anything beyond "responding to God" becomes manipulation. David understood this. Saul had been anointed as king by Samuel.[116] But Saul's pride and rebellion had caused God to take the kingship from him. David had then been anointed by Samuel.[117] So there were two "anointeds", but only one could rule. Saul's jealousy drove him to seek to kill David. David's honor of his King and trust in God's

---

[114] *Song of Solomon*, The Art of Conflict

[115] Could this really be what Jesus had in mind when He said, "Judge not . . ." in Luke 6:37 (the most abused passage of our day)? It certainly has replaced John 3:16 as the most remembered, especially by those acting in ways they know to be wrong.

[116] First Samuel 9

[117] First Samuel 16

providence compelled him to twice forego golden opportunities to kill Saul and secure what God had indeed given to him.[118]

Somewhere around the time of the writing of First Peter, Peter's fellow apostle, Paul, is finishing up his Third Missionary Journey and headed back to Jerusalem[119]. Three times on the trip back, Paul is warned that bad things are about to happen when he arrives in Jerusalem. His brothers and sisters prophesy and plead with him not to go. Paul's response?

"Why are you weeping and breaking my heart? I am ready not only to be bound, but also to die in Jerusalem for the name of the Lord Jesus." (Acts 21:13, NIV)

Paul got it. No fight or flight. He knew **the most important thing.**

Peter got it.

David got it.

Do you see a pattern here?

---

[118] First Samuel 24 & 26
[119] Acts 21

??? QUESTIONS FOR REFLECTION

- When does the most important thing not become the most important thing?
- What would have been the "rational, commonsense" decision for Paul regarding going to Jerusalem? Wouldn't it make more sense for him to avoid death, live on and preach to and convert more people?
- Should my behavior toward someone depend on the behavior of that other person?
- Is there a point at which Peter says that submission is to cease? Is there a point at which the abuse/torture/execution becomes unacceptably severe? Is there an act so egregious that one is no longer called to surrender/submit/serve/sacrifice? If not, why not? If so, who decides?

THIRTEEN

THE SLAVE

First Peter 2:18-20

"He is no fool who gives what he cannot keep
to gain what he cannot lose."[120]

---

[120] Jim Elliott, Journal, October 28, 1949

·· 13 ··

Peter's nowhere close to being through, yet. He now brings it down a level, to slaves. And he repeats one of our "s" words: submit.

But now, Peter ratchets it up a notch. He even answers our question in the previous chapter about whether he mistakenly forgot to tell us to only submit to "good" kings. He removes all doubt as he talks about submitting "with all respect" to masters:

"Slaves, submit yourselves to your masters with all respect, not only to those who are good and considerate, **but also to those who are harsh**. For it is commendable if a man bears up under the pain of **unjust** suffering because he is conscious of God." (I Peter 2:18-19, NIV)

We're talking about bad, mean, abusive masters here.

And Peter anticipates the question.

"But how is it to your credit if you receive a beating for doing wrong and endure it?" (I Peter 2:20a, NIV)

Peter is asking, "What's the big deal if you misbehave and get beaten for it. That's just. You should be punished. That's right and it's fair. That's the way it's supposed to happen."

"But if you suffer for doing good and you endure it, this is commendable before God." (I Peter 2:20b, NIV)

You mean, Peter, that if I'm abused for doing nothing, I'm to just sit there and take it?

Actually, no. Peter says that if you get abused "for doing **good**" (not for doing nothing), you endure it.

Where is fight or flight?

Of all of my heroes of the faith, there are none that impact me more than the five missionaries to the Waodani tribe in Ecuador. While many know their story, I have to assume that some readers don't. So, let me share with you this wonderful story of total self-sacrifice.

On January 8, 1956, when I was only two years old, five young men sat on a sand bar in the Curaray River in the jungles of Ecuador. Jim Elliot, Nate Saint, Roger Youdarian, Pete Fleming, and Ed McCulley had been called to evangelize a savage tribe, the Waodanis. All previous attempts to make contact with this tribe had ended in death for those making the attempt, whether missionaries, oil explorers, or trappers. The Waodanis were legendary for their seven-foot spears. In fact, the primary cause of death in the tribe was murder by spearing. (They were also called "Auca" for "savage.")

These young missionaries were all in their twenties and thirties, with wives and children. In the prime of life. Prior to going to Ecuador, Nate Saint was asked if they would use the guns they were taking for hunting food to defend themselves if they were attacked.

His response is one that Peter or Paul could have made:

"No. They're not ready for heaven. We are."

And before the sun set on the Curaray River on that Lord's Day in 1956, all five men had been speared to death, their bodies floating in the river, their brides widowed, their children fatherless.

These men are my heroes. I have a copy of the January 30, 1956 issue of *Life* magazine, which contains a photoessay of the martyrdom of these men. They became known as "The Auca Five."

So where was fight or flight for these missionaries?

That decision, that commitment, that surrender was made long before that Sunday on a sand bar in Ecuador. These men knew the answer to the question,

"What's **the most important thing**?"

Nate Saint knew the answer: "They're not ready for heaven. We are."

?⁇? QUESTIONS FOR REFLECTION

- Does Nate's response only apply to the Waodanis?
- Does this only apply to missionaries?
- Does this only apply to murderous savages?
- What was more important, the physical lives of the Auca Five? Or the eternal lives of the Waodanis?
- Is there any situation in which it does not apply?

Hold on to that last question as we drill down deeper.

FOURTEEN

THE SAVIOR

First Peter 2:21-25

In the midst of horrific persecution . . . murder,
torture, forced conversion, human trafficking, millions of
Christians have fled ISIS-controlled Iraq. Yet, thousands
remained, risking all they have in this world, including
their very lives. They were asked why? Their response:
"The Muslims need us."[121]

---

[121] Mindy Belz, *They Say We Are Infidels*

·· 14 ··

Peter knows what we're thinking. He knows that we're thinking, "Seriously?!?" And not just, "Seriously?", but "How far does he want us to take this?" He was thinking the same thing at one time. But that was pre-Pentecost. That was before the Holy Spirit. And rather than exert his apostolic authority to tell us how serious he is, Peter appeals to the ultimate Authority and Example, not for us to see how He *would* handle it, but to see how He *did* handle it.

Read it . . . and yes, weep.

". . . Christ suffered for you, leaving you an example, that you should follow in His steps. 'He committed no sin, and no deceit was found in His mouth.' When they hurled their insults at Him, He did not retaliate; when He suffered, He made no threats." (I Peter 2:21b-23, NIV)

Ouch.

Do you see why I said that God just kept hemming me in?

What was Jesus's mission? (Maybe if His were different, it'll give us some way to get out of this!)

Well, we don't have to wonder. Listen to Him:

"The hour has come for the Son of Man to be glorified. I tell you the truth, unless a kernel of wheat falls to the ground and dies, it remains only a single seed. But if it dies, it produces many seeds. The man who loves his life will lose it, while the man who hates his life in this world will keep it for eternal life. Whoever serves me must follow me; and where I am, my servant also will be. My Father will honor the one who serves me.

Now my heart is troubled, and what shall I say? 'Father, save me from this hour'? No, **it was for this very reason I came to this hour**. Father, glorify Your name!" (John 12: 23-28, NIV)

Peter got this better than anyone.

We all remember when Jesus rebuked Peter with "Get thee behind me, Satan!" (Mark 8:33b, NIV) But do we remember *why* Jesus rebuked Peter?

In the preceding verses, Jesus had told the disciples what was about to happen, that He would be killed. Scripture tells us that "He spoke plainly about this, and Peter took Him aside and began to rebuke Him." (Mark 8:32, NIV)

That's when Jesus rebuked Peter, and followed that rebuke with, "You do not have in mind the things of God, but the things of men." (Mark 8:32c, NIV)

"Then He called the crowd to Him along with His disciples and said: 'If anyone would come after me, he must deny himself and take up his cross and follow me. For whoever wants to save his life will lose it, but whoever loses his life for me and for the gospel will save it. What good is it for a man to gain the whole world, yet forfeit his soul? Or what can a man give in exchange for his soul?'" (Mark 8:33b-37)

No. His mission was the same as ours.

"He Himself bore our sins in His body on the tree, so that we might die to sins and live for righteousness: by His wounds you have been healed." (I Peter 2:24, NIV)

The most important thing to Jesus was (is!) that He see us on the other side.

Nothing.

Else.

Mattered.

Even to the death.

And notice that I left off the preface to Peter's example of Jesus' selflessness (even to the death). The phrase that is bracketed by the example of a slave enduring unjust suffering on one side, and the example of Jesus' crucifixion on the other side is,

"To this you were called . . ." (I Peter 2:21a, NIV)

Bruce Chen understood that calling.[122]

Ernest Gordon's comrade understood that calling.[123]

The Auca Five understood that calling.[124]

Peter understood that calling. He heard Jesus say, "Greater love hath no man than this, that a man lay down his life for his friends."[125]

Peter . . . and Bruce Chen . . . and Ernest Gordon's comrade . . . and Jim and Nate and Roger and Pete and Ed . . . and God . . . they just keep hemming me in . . .

And the hits just keep on comin' . . .

O Love That Will Not Let Me Go[126]

O Love that will not let me go,
I rest my weary soul in thee;
I give thee back the life I owe,
That in thine ocean depths its flow
May richer, fuller be.

O light that followest all my way,
I yield my flickering torch to thee;
My heart restores its borrowed ray,
That in thy sunshine's blaze its day
May brighter, fairer be.

O Joy that seekest me through pain,
I cannot close my heart to thee;
I trace the rainbow through the rain,

---

122 Chapter Three
123 Chapter Five
124 Chapter Thirteen
125 John 15:13 (KJV)
126 Lyrics: George Matheson (1882); Music: Albert Peace (1884), Public Domain

And feel the promise is not vain,
That morn shall tearless be.

O Cross that liftest up my head,
I dare not ask to fly from thee;
I lay in dust life's glory dead,
And from the ground there blossoms red
Life that shall endless be.

⁇ QUESTIONS FOR REFLECTION

- Do you suppose that any of the most egregious acts were not being suffered by those people that Peter addressed in his letter?
- Is my mission any different than that of those who have died because of their Christianity, e.g. the five missionaries?
- Is my continued life on this earth any more important or valuable than that of those who have died because they simply acted like Jesus?

FIFTEEN

THE WIFE

First Peter 3:1-6

"You're never more like Jesus than when you're in
submission . . . and you're never more like the
devil than when you're in rebellion."[127]

---

[127] Dr. Adrian Rogers

·· 15 ··

If you think that it's been challenging so far, just wait. Now Peter brings the personal nature of that challenge down to another level. He now gets into an area that affects the majority of us: marriage.

Ladies first.

Meet Fred E. Mashburn, Jr.[128], one of my heroes of the faith.

But it wasn't always so. Soon after Fred married Bette Jo, they quickly had four children. Bette Jo was a believer; Fred was not.

But Fred liked to fish . . . even on Sundays. Especially on Sundays.

And they only had one car.

So, Fred took the car and went fishing. And Bette Jo let Fred take the car. So she walked with four little children to church . . . Sunday morning . . . Sunday night . . . come rain . . . come shine . . . come sleet . . . come snow . . . every week.

As Peter begins his address to the wives, watch the phrase he uses: "Wives, in the same way be submissive to your husbands . . ." (I Peter 3:1a, NIV)

Well, the first thing we've got to ask is, "In the same way as what?"

And looking back, the answer becomes (painfully) obvious:

- In the same way as the abused, crucified Jesus
- In the same way as abused slaves
- In the same way as abused, martyred citizens of a murderous king

The next question that comes to mind is similar to the question we asked during our discussion of the call to submit to, honor, and respect the king. Does Peter mean to submit to all husbands, or just the good ones?

While he doesn't go into quite the detail that he did with masters, we get some good hints that he means *all* husbands, good and bad. First, the "in the same way" qualifier refers to the three examples before husbands . . . and that includes the example of those who crucified Jesus, good masters and bad masters, good kings and bad kings.

Second, while it's not a given that unbelieving husbands are worse than

---

[128] 1927-2012; Founding Elder, Northwest Church of Christ, Durant, Oklahoma. (A quote from him introduced Chapter Eight)

believing husbands, Peter specifically addresses the wives of unbelievers, and that their behavior might win over their unbelieving husbands. And one would have to believe that there might be a few bad apples in that bunch.

But once again, Peter reinforces the answer to the question, "What's **the most important thing**?" with the reason for the wife's submission: ". . . so that, if any of them do not believe the word, they may be won over without words by the behavior of the wives, when they see the purity and reverence of your lives." (I Peter 3:1b-2, NIV)

The. Most. Important. Thing. Is that you see the person God has placed in front of you on the other side.

Even if it's an abusive husband?

Time out.

OK, Dear Reader. If you've been with me thus far . . . if you've stayed with the thought process so far, my guess is that this is the point in the book where you leave me. You can see where this is going and you don't like it.

Neither do I.

But before you leave, before you think that I'm some sort of a misogynist, male chauvinist pig, let me just say a couple of things.

First, let me remind you (and myself) that I have three beautiful daughters . . . and five beautiful granddaughters. And if any husband abused them, I'd be the first to defend those women.

Second, you won't find me telling any woman what to do in their particular case. What we're going to do here is simply follow the evidence and see where it leads.

So, stay with me for a while.

> "Your beauty should not come from outward adornment, such as braided hair and the wearing of gold jewelry and fine clothes. Instead, it should be that of your inner self, the unfading beauty of a gentle and quiet spirit, which is of great worth in God's sight. For this is the way the holy women of the past who put their hope in God used to make themselves beautiful. They were submissive to their own husbands, like Sarah, who obeyed Abraham

and called him her master. You are her daughters if you do what is right and do not give way to fear." (I Peter 3:3-8, NIV)

Peter goes on to extol "the unfading beauty of a gentle and quiet spirit, which is of great worth in God's sight." He then compares those who do submit and behave to Sarah, and encourages them to "do what is right and not give way to fear."

Let's stop for a minute and camp on that last phrase. Why would they give way to fear? And what would they have to fear?

If you ask most people what they fear most, you'll get a variety of answers, from spiders, to the dark, to roller coasters. But eventually, at the top of most folks' list is death. Makes sense, doesn't it? After all, we spend an inordinate amount of money trying to stave off death. Health care accounts for eighteen percent of the national gross domestic product (and rising), so we're spending an awful lot to keep from dying!

In any given situation, what's the worst thing that can happen? We can die, right? And, at the end of the day, that fear produces selfishness. After all, it is about **self**-preservation.

But for the believer, what happens when we die?

We see Jesus face to face!!!!!

Not a bad gig, is it . . .

In thinking back to the story of the five Aucan missionaries, can we revive some questions? Hard questions?

Which is more important, the physical lives of the five missionaries, or the eternal lives of the Waodanis?

Which is more important, the physical well-being (or life) of a wife, or the eternal life of her husband?

Were those five missionaries fools for doing what they did?

Well, the rest of the story may affect your answer.

After the deaths of Jim Elliot, Nate Saint, Roger Youdarian, Ed McCulley, and Pete Fleming, Jim's widow, Elisabeth, and Nate's sister, Rachel, returned to the Waodanis, eventually converting them to Christ. Years later, Nate's son and daughter were baptized in the Curaray River in the very place where their father was murdered. The man who baptized them? Mincaye, the Waodani who murdered their father.

Dawa, one of the Waodani women converted by Elisabeth Elliot and Rachel Saint, quoted First Peter 2:21-24 in her language:

"Being speared Himself, God's one and only Son did not spear back. He let Himself be killed, so the people killing Him would one day live well."

But wait. There's more.

One year after the loss of their husbands, the widows of the "Auca Five" wrote a prayer:

"Our hearts are filled with gratitude for the privilege He gave us in being the wives of men who were chosen to be slain for His sake. None of us is worthy. It is all of His grace, but we know that the Lamb is worthy, a thousand times, the lives of our husbands and of us. He chose to glorify Himself in their death—may He now glorify Himself in our lives.

Not only do we ask that Christ be glorified in the Aucas and in us, but also in our children. Most of them will have no recollection of their fine fathers. But our Lord gave His word, 'All the children shall be taught of the Lord, and great shall be the peace of the children.' We ask for His wisdom in training them, for His Spirit in us, that they may be as obedient as their fathers. How wonderful it would be if He should prepare one or more of them to go to the Aucas! We would give them to Him for his use, asking that they come to know Him as Savior and Lord at an early age. Far be it from us to withhold from the Lord the lives of these little ones, children of the men who did not withhold their own lives. May they sing from true hearts,

Faith of our Fathers,
Holy faith
We would be true
to Thee till death."[129]

Selflessness. Total selflessness. Even to the death.

Jesus's calling.

Our calling.

So how do we respond? How should we then live?

It's not my place to tell a woman to stay with an abusive man, any more than it's my place to tell anyone to go to the jungles of Ecuador unarmed and make contact with murderous savages.

All we can do is read the Word, hear the voice of God, and seek to understand and reflect His nature to a lost and (eternally) dying world.

Fred and Bette Jo? Well, you've already figured it out. As Fred watched "the purity and reverence of" Bette Jo's life; when he saw "the unfading beauty of a gentle and quiet spirit", he was "won over." His quote introduced Chapter 8 of this book. And countless lives have been influenced for Jesus, lives that you and I will see on the other side, all because of that man . . . and a woman who answered the call.

The call may be clear. Answering that call is up to each of us.

---

[129] *Christianity Today*, January 7, 1957, pp. 6-8

⁇ MORE REFLECTIVE QUESTIONS

- Is a despot king any different from the Waodani?
- How about a mean boss ("master")?
- How about those who crucified Jesus?
- How about a betraying business partner?
- How about whoever it is that "done you wrong?"
- How about a bad spouse?
- How about an adulterous spouse?
- How about an abusive spouse?
- Why did Peter put this section into his letter?
- Why did he continue to insert the phrase "in the same way"?
- Were there abused women in Peter's first century audience?
- Why did Peter not qualify his admonition to submit?
- Whose physical life is more valuable? Each of the Aucan Five missionaries? Or an abused wife?
- What if it's your daughter . . . or granddaughter?

SIXTEEN

THE HUSBAND

First Peter 3:7

"It's not love that holds your marriage together . . .
it's your marriage that holds your love together."[130]

---

[130] Dr. Adrian Rogers

Now that Peter has addressed the women, he turns to the men. And once again, the phrase "in the same way" rears its ugly head. OK. It's not an ugly head; it's just a head that keeps hemming us in. In reality, Peter uses this phrase to make clear what he's trying to say, and that the expectation that follows applies to every person who is called, in every relationship.

. . . in the same way as what?

in the same way as citizens of a despot king,

in the same way as slaves of an unjust master,

in the same way as a tortured, crucified Savior,

in the same way as a submissive wife.

> "Husbands, in the same way be considerate as you live with your wives, and treat them with respect as the weaker partner and as heirs with you of the gracious gift of life, so that nothing will hinder your prayers." (I Peter 3:7, NIV)

Without question, husbands have the higher calling. They are to give their lives for their brides. Paul makes this clear in his discourse to husbands in the Ephesian letter, where he says, "Husbands, love (*agapao*) your wives, just as Christ loved the church **and gave Himself up for her** . . ." (Ephesians 5:25, NIV) The call is for the husband to "agape" his bride, to do what is in the best interest of the wife, even if it costs him . . . even if it costs him his life, just as it cost Jesus' life for His bride, the church.

In his earlier letter to the Corinthians, in making his case for remaining unmarried, Paul says that "a married man is concerned about the affairs of this world – how he can please his wife . . ." (I Corinthian 7:33, NIV) Paul's assumption is the "agape" of husband to wife. The husband's concern/desire/obligation is to do what is in the best interest of his wife . . . as Christ did (and does) for His bride, the church. The "agape" is assumed.

When Peter refers to the wife as the "weaker partner", he doesn't mean inferior. I love the description Tommy Nelson uses in his Song of Solomon video series. Using the KJV "weaker vessel" he compares the wife to a fine crystal goblet or a fine china cup, as contrasted with an iron skillet. All are vessels, containers. We treat the former with special care, often displaying them in a prominent place in the house, unlike the latter, which we bang around with little or no care, and keep hidden in a drawer or lower counter.

Likewise, husbands are to treat their wives with the same care and honor that we would those special "weaker" vessels compared above. More so, *agape* compels them to "esteem others better than themselves"[131], most of all, their wives, their partner.

Then Peter just makes the calling even more consequential when he tells us that if we (men) aren't loving our wives with *agape* love, it messes with our prayers! This makes sense in light of what Peter's fellow disciple and business partner says. His buddy John writes in his first letter that "whoever does not love their brother and sister, whom they have seen, cannot love God, whom they have not seen. And He has given us this command: Anyone who loves God must also love their brother and sister." (I John 4:20b-21, NIV)

Peter understood that if we aren't showing *agape* love toward our sister (in this case our wife, which heightens the criticality even more!), we can't have an *agape* relationship with the Father. Put another way, one can't have a right relationship with Jesus and a wrong relationship with his wife. Ouch!

It goes without saying that, just as there are bad husbands around, there are some crummy wives out there, too. Some who are unworthy of having selflessness shown toward them.

So what?

The worthiness of the loved does not dictate the behavior of the lover. Jesus dictates that behavior.

Just ask Roberto[132]. Married to Selina[133] for twenty years, they were the parents of four children. Each morning before dawn, Roberto would leave their small, Central American home to work on a farm for four dollars a day. Each night, he would come home after dark where Selina would have a meal of rice and tortillas prepared for her husband. But each night for twenty years, Selina would wait until Roberto entered the door and

---

[131] Philippians 2:3 (NIV)

[132] Not his real name

[133] Not her real name

looked on his plate. Then, as she caught his eye, she would take the meal and throw it into the fire.

Roberto was a Christian. And Selina despised him for it.

But Roberto is a hero.

Each night, as he watched his bride's repeated act of disgust, Roberto would smile, lay down his tools, and play with his children. Night after night, those children witnessed their mother prepare a meal for their father, knowing full well that the intent of the meal was part of an act of contempt and irreverence. For nearly twenty years, each day brought with it an expectation of disrespect and derision displayed at the climax of the day.

And each day, Roberto surrendered his will to that of his Master. Roberto showed Selina *agape* love. He stayed the course. He did what was in her best interest . . . even if it cost him. Until finally, God brought just the right person into Selina's life. And He changed her heart. Selina surrendered her life to Jesus. And today, husband and wife are united in Christ.

And God continues to redeem them and their family.

"This is a profound mystery – but I am talking about Christ and the church." (Ephesians 5:32, NIV)

"God created human marriage to reveal the love relationship between Christ and His bride."[134]

Jesus's bride mistreats Him;

Jesus's bride abuses Him;

Jesus's bride prostitutes herself with others.

BUT,

Jesus remains faithful;

Jesus shows His (*agape*) love for her;

Jesus is selfless;

Jesus gives His life for her.

In a culture where men are divorcing and deserting their wives in record numbers, Peter calls us to stay the course to show Jesus' love for

---

[134] Randy Alcorn, *Heaven*

and treatment of His bride. He calls husbands to make whatever sacrifice necessary for their brides. He calls them to give their lives for them.

In a culture where men are acting like little boys . . . little babies to be more precise, Peter calls on men to man up. He challenges them to the calling of Christ to be the spiritual leader of their family, no matter the cost. He calls us to regain our legacy of "women and children first."

And Peter's not through.

??? QUESTION FOR REFLECTION

- Is my continued life on this earth worth more than the eternal soul of any human being? If so, which one?

SEVENTEEN

THE FEAR

First Peter 3:8-18

"Let thy hope of heaven master thy fear of death."[135]

---

[135] William Gurnall, English author and Anglican clergyman (1616-1679)

·· 17 ··

On March 12, 2005, Ashley Smith was taken hostage in her home by Brian Nichols in Atlanta. The previous day, Nichols overpowered an Atlanta courthouse deputy as he was being escorted to court for a rape trial March 11. He then shot and killed the presiding judge and a court reporter before killing another deputy as he left the courthouse. Later he killed a federal agent in an attempt to flee authorities. Escaping, he became the subject of the largest manhunt in Georgia history.

Bound by Nichols, Ashley asked if she could get a book she was reading. Granted that request, she got her Bible and a copy of The Purpose Driven Life[136] *and read to him.*

She asked, "Do you believe in miracles? Because if you don't believe in miracles -- you are here for a reason. You're here in my apartment for some reason. You got out of that courthouse with police everywhere, and you don't think that's a miracle? You don't think you're supposed to be sitting right here in front of me listening to me tell you, you know, your reason here?"

Ashley then said, "You know, your miracle could be that you need to -- you need to be caught for this." She continued, "You need to go to prison and you need to share the Word of God with them, with all the prisoners there."

Allowed by Nichols to leave to pick up her daughter, Smith escaped. Nichols surrendered and was sentenced to multiple life sentences without possibility of parole.

Well, Peter has lined up one relationship after another:

- Citizen of a despot king
- Slave of an unjust master
- Executed Messiah of a mob
- Wife of an abusive husband
- Husband of an abusive wife

And he now comes to "Finally . . ." This must be the wrap up. Or is it? While Peter is not through, he is going to tie a little bit of a bow on what he's revealed to us up to this point. While he doesn't use the phrase

---

[136] Rick Warren

"in the same way", he does pull it together with that word of conclusion: finally. Then, as if to say, "If I've missed any relationships in the previous group, I'm about to include you . . . all of you.

> "Finally, all of you, live in harmony with one another; be sympathetic, love as brothers, be compassionate and humble. Do not repay evil with evil of insult with insult, but with blessings, because to this you were called so that you may inherit a blessing." (I Peter 3:8-9, NIV)

But Peter not only pulls the audience together, he also pulls the two thoughts together:

1. Behave like Jesus.
2. Suffer like Jesus.

First, he gets specific with the behavior:

- Live in harmony
- Be sympathetic
- Love as brothers
- Be compassionate
- Be humble
- Don't repay evil with evil
- Don't repay insult with insult
- Repay evil and insult with blessing

Peter then reminds us as readers, "to this you were (and here's that word again) called."[137] And then he quotes the thirty-fourth Psalm.
"For,

'Whoever would love life
and see good days must keep his tongue from evil
and his lips from deceitful speech.
He must turn from evil and do good;

---

[137] I Peter 3:9b

he must seek peace and pursue it.
For the eyes of the Lord are on the
righteous
and His ears are attentive to their
prayer,
but the face of the Lord is against those
who do evil.'"
(I Peter 3:10-12, NIV)

My minister son-in-law[138] once wondered aloud to me if, perhaps, Peter could have been meditating on this passage as he dictated to Silas.[139] Peter then turns to the second thought: suffering.

- He knows of their suffering.
- He knows of their fear and pain and loss.
- He knows of their fear of death.

So, he asks their question.

"Who is going to harm you if you are eager to do good? But even if you should suffer for what is right, you are blessed." (I Peter 3:13-14a, NIV)

He continues to reinforce the thought that **they will suffer for doing right, for doing good**; and that there is blessing in suffering.

And when Peter once again addresses the issue of not being afraid, he points to "what they (unbelievers) fear."

"Do not fear what they fear; do not be frightened." (I Peter 3:14b, NIV)

The Hebrew writer, in talking about Jesus, tells about how He came to "free those who all their lives were held in slavery by their fear of death." (Hebrews 2:15, NIV) That's it! The unbeliever is held in slavery by their fear of death. But Peter says not to fear death as they do. Peter heard Jesus say, "Do not be afraid of those who kill the body, but cannot kill the soul." (Matthew 10:28, NIV)

---

[138] Aaron Loney, Pulpit Minister, Weatherford, Oklahoma Church of Christ
[139] I Peter 5:12

Oswald Chambers[140] said, "The remarkable thing about God is that when you fear God, you fear nothing else; whereas, if you do not fear God, you fear everything else." Why? Because death is not the end for the believer; it's the beginning of eternity with Jesus . . . face to face! Once again, not a bad gig . . .

And how is that fear conquered?

"But in your hearts set apart Christ as Lord." (I Peter 3:15a, NIV)

Can we break down those last three words?

Christ (Gr. *Christos*) is the Greek word for the Hebrew title, Messiah: "anointed one." (Growing up, I always thought that was Jesus' last name; you know, Lord Jesus Christ.)

And in our democratic culture where we have no ruling class, no nobility, and (at least, in theory) no classes in our society, we don't even think about the word "lord" as being descriptive of someone. But in reality, the word carries the meaning of someone in authority, a nobleman, someone in charge.

So what Peter is actually saying in this imperative is for us to internalize Jesus (the Christ or Messiah) as the ruler of our lives. He becomes the boss, the king, the ruler, the master, the one who tells us what to do and how to do it.

Jesus determines our behavior.

Not the world.

Not the culture.

Not the behavior of the person in front of us.

And that behavior (as exemplified by Jesus, and specified in the earlier verses[141]) will be counter-cultural.

And once again, this causes Peter to anticipate the next move. He juxtaposes the counter-cultural behavior of the believer (who, as a reminder, is on a mission!) with that of the unbelieving world they find themselves in.

> "Always be prepared to give an answer to everyone who asks you to give the reason for the hope that you have. But do this with gentleness and respect, keeping a clear conscience, so that those who speak maliciously against

---

[140] 1874-1917; from *My Utmost for His Highest*

[141] I Peter 3:8-9

your good behavior in Christ may be ashamed of their slander." (I Peter 3:15b-16, NIV)

This verse has been a cornerstone verse in my tribe[142] for as long as I can remember. It has been misused to compel us to have the right answer on all things doctrinal, from baptism to communion to music.

No, no, no . . .

That's not what Peter has in mind at all here.

The reason Peter tells his readers to "be prepared to give an answer to everyone who asks you to give the reason for the hope that you have" (I Peter 3:15b, NIV) has nothing to do with doctrine. Peter is saying this:

If you are self-controlled,[143]

If you rid yourself of all malice,

If you rid yourself of all deceit,

If you rid yourself of all hypocrisy,

If you rid yourself of all envy,

If you rid yourself of all slander,[144]

If you abstain from sinful desires,[145]

If you don't conform to evil desires,[146]

If you submit to a despot king who tortures and kills you,[147]

If you submit to masters who punish you even when you do right,[148]

If you follow your Lord and don't retaliate when insulted,

If you don't threaten when beaten,[149]

If you are submissive to your husband (even when he is not good to you),

If you honor and revere your wife as your partner (even when she is not good to you),

If you are sympathetic

If you are compassionate,

---

[142] Churches of Christ, descendants of the Restoration Movement

[143] 1:13

[144] 2:1

[145] 2:11

[146] 1:14

[147] 2:13-17

[148] 2:18-20

[149] 2:23

If you are humble,
If you don't repay evil with evil,
If you don't repay insult with insult,
If you repay evil and insult with blessing,[150]
If you are eager to do good,
If you suffer for what is right,[151]
If you behave as Jesus (your King, the One who called you),
Then, my friend . . .

---

[150] 3:8-9
[151] 3:13-14

You.

Look.

Weird.

And the world around you will look on you and ask, why?!?

What is it about you that makes you take what you take, act as a doormat[152], willing to go to the death, and yet do so with joy in your heart and blessing on your lips for your persecutors?

THEN . . .

then, you tell them about the One who died for you. Then you tell them that He died for them, as well. Then you tell them about the One who made life worth living and allows you to face death with hope and assurance. Then you tell them about the One who can set them free from slavery to sin, the One who can take away the pain of this life and replace it with joy. Then you tell them that this One who came to die for them[153] was God, was resurrected[154], and is God. Then you tell the world that He loves them.[155]

And when they see you and hear of Him, as the centurion did as he saw the sacrifice of Jesus, may they join with him in proclaiming, "Surely He was the Son of God!" (Matthew 27:54, NIV)

That is your mission.

That is your life's purpose

That, my friend, is **the most important thing**.

One hundred years from now . . . nothing else will matter.

That's why Peter can say, "It is better, if it is God's will, to suffer for doing good than for doing evil." (I Peter 3:17, NIV) Peter knew it. He lived it. No more fight or flight.

Peter then seals that with a parenthetical reassurance for his readers that their salvation is sealed and that even the spirits know this. Jesus proclaimed it to the disobedient ones, and now is seen by all spiritual beings at God's right hand.

---

[152] Definition: Doormat: "a person who is the habitual object of abuse or humiliation by another. a person who offers little resistance to ill-treatment by others. a person who is regularly and predictably exploited by others; constant victim." Sound like Anybody we know?

[153] I Peter 3:18a

[154] I Peter 3:18b

[155] John 3:16

"For Christ died for sins once for all, the righteous for the unrighteous, to bring you to God. He was put to death in the body but made alive by the Spirit, through whom also He went and preached to the spirits in prison who disobeyed long ago when God waited patiently in the days of Noah while the ark was being built. In it only a few people, eight in all, were saved through water, and this water symbolizes baptism that now saves you also – not the removal of dirt from the body but the pledge of a good conscience toward God. It saves you by the resurrection of Jesus Christ, who has gone into heaven and is at God's right hand – with angels, authorities, and powers in submission to Him." (I Peter 3:18-22, NIV)

Jesus conquered death and we can face death with the confidence that it is not final. And therein lies the joy that the world finds so unbelievable.

Only one such as Elisabeth Elliot[156] could speak with the kind of authority that she does:

"Anything, if offered to God, can become a gateway to joy."

---

[156] (1926-2015) Widow of Jim Elliot

⁇ MORE REFLECTIVE QUESTIONS

- Was Ashley Smith a fool for sharing Jesus with Brian Nichols? Would she have been a fool if she had lost her life? Does your knowledge of the outcome change your answer?
- What is it that "they" (pagans) fear?
- How about me? Do I fear the same thing?
- Why would anyone "ask you to give the reason for the hope that you have?" If they haven't asked me, what does that say about me? My behavior?

EIGHTEEN

THE ATTITUDE

First Peter 4:1-11

"The Sermon on the Mount indicates that, when we are on a mission for Jesus Christ, there is no time to stand up for ourselves. Jesus says, in effect, 'Don't worry about whether or not you are being treated justly.' Looking for justice is actually a sign that we have been diverted from our devotion to Him. Never look for justice in this world, but never cease to give it."[157]

---

[157] Oswald Chambers, *My Utmost for His Highest*, June 27

$$\cdot\cdot \ 18 \ \cdot\cdot$$

On October 2, 2006, a shooting occurred at the West Nickel Mines School. Gunman Charles Carl Roberts IV took hostages and shot eight out of ten girls, killing five, before committing suicide in the schoolhouse. His wife, Marie, returned home from a prayer study group and received a phone call from her husband just prior to initiating the shooting.

On the day of the shooting, a grandfather of one of the murdered Amish girls was heard warning some young relatives not to hate the killer, saying, "We must not think evil of this man." Another Amish father noted, "He had a mother and a wife and a soul and now he's standing before a just God." Jack Meyer, a member of the Brethren community living near the Amish in Lancaster County, explained: "I don't think there's anybody here that wants to do anything but forgive and not only reach out to those who have suffered a loss in that way, but to reach out to the family of the man who committed these acts."

A Roberts family spokesman said an Amish neighbor comforted the Roberts family hours after the shooting and extended forgiveness to them. Amish community members visited and comforted Roberts' widow, parents, and parents-in-law. One Amish man held Roberts' sobbing father in his arms, reportedly for as long as an hour, to comfort him. The Amish have also set up a charitable fund for the family of the shooter. About thirty members of the Amish community attended Roberts' funeral, and Marie Roberts, the widow of the killer, was one of the few outsiders invited to the funeral of one of the victims.

Marie Roberts wrote an open letter to her Amish neighbors thanking them for their forgiveness, grace, and mercy. She wrote, "Your love for our family has helped to provide the healing we so desperately need. Gifts you've given have touched our hearts in a way no words can describe. Your compassion has reached beyond our family, beyond our community, and is changing our world, and for this we sincerely thank you."[158]

One would think that Peter had made his point and had come to a good place to stop. But not Peter. And his readers are the beneficiaries of his overflow.

---

[158] From the Wikipedia account. The movie "Amish Grace" is based on this event.

Once more he begins it with a "therefore."

> "Therefore, since Christ suffered in His body, arm
> yourselves also with the same attitude, because he who has
> suffered in his body is done with sin." (I Peter 4:1, NIV)

And the "therefore" ties directly back into 3:18, where he tells us that it's better, if it's God's will, to suffer for doing good than for doing evil . . . so did Christ[159]. He then picks up that since He suffered in His body (and we may, as well), we should arm ourselves with the same attitude[160].

There can be no better picture of the attitude of Christ than that portrayed by Paul in Philippians, and it absolutely reinforces the sacrificial, selfless, submissive attitude that Peter is urging his readers to imitate:

> "If you have any encouragement from being united with
> Christ,
> if any comfort from His love,
> if any fellowship with the Spirit,
> if any tenderness and compassion,
> then make my joy complete by being like-minded,
> having the same love,
> being one in spirit and purpose.
>
> Do nothing out of selfish ambition or vain conceit, but in
> humility consider others better than yourselves. Each of
> you should look not only to your own interests, but also
> to the interests of others.
>
> **Your attitude should be the same as that of Christ
> Jesus:**
>
> Who, being in very nature God, did not consider equality
> with God something to be grasped, but made Himself
> nothing, taking the very nature of a servant, being made

---

[159] I Peter 3:17-18
[160] I Peter 4:1

in human likeness. And being found in appearance as a man, He humbled Himself and became obedient to death – even death on a cross." (Philippians 2:1-8, NIV)

But is Peter talking only about Jesus' attitude?

In the context of Peter's multiple prior "in the same ways", could Peter also be alluding not only to the primary reference (Jesus), but to the earlier relationships as well?

Same attitude as:

- All of you[161]
- Husbands[162]
- Wives[163]
- Jesus[164]
- Slaves of an abusive master[165]
- Citizens of an abusive king[166]

Peter then tells us that when we suffer for Christ, it makes it so much harder for us to go into sin. Remember, we're not of this world anyway: aliens . . . strangers . . . called . . . elect . . . holy. And listen to Peter describe us, how (we) "do not live the rest of (our) **earthly lives** for **evil human desires**, but rather for the will of God." (I Peter 4:2, NIV)

That is our purpose, our reason for being.

This is our calling.

> "For you have spent enough time in the past doing what pagans choose to do – living in debauchery, lust, drunkenness, orgies, carousing and detestable idolatry." (I Peter 4:3, NIV)

Peter then details a laundry list of those evil human desires, followed

---

[161] I Peter 3:8
[162] I Peter 3:7
[163] I Peter 3:1
[164] I Peter 2:21
[165] I Peter 2:18
[166] I Peter 2:13

by one more contrast between the counter-cultural behavior of those who are called and the abuse from those who are dying:

> "They think it strange that you do not plunge with them into the same flood of dissipation, and they heap abuse on you." (I Peter 4:4, NIV)

Sounds very much like the culture we now live in, doesn't it?

> "But they will have to give account to Him who is ready to judge the living and the dead. For this is the reason the gospel was preached even to those who are now dead, so that they might be judged according to men in regard to the body, but live according to God in regard to the spirit." (I Peter 4:5-6, NIV)

And, because of the contrast, remember . . . you will look weird! And Peter just doesn't get off message.

> "The end of all things is near. Therefore, be clear minded and self-controlled so that you can pray. Above all, love each other deeply, because love covers over a multitude of sins." (I Peter 4:7-8)

When Peter says that "love covers over a multitude of sins," whose sins is he talking about? Remember, it's *agape* he's talking about. So, the sins that my *agape* covers are those of the one who sinned against me! "Where love (agape) abounds, offenses are frequently overlooked and quickly forgotten."[167]

Think Jesus![168]

> "Offer hospitality to one another without grumbling. Each one should use whatever gift he has received to serve others, faithfully administering God's grace in its various

---

[167] ESV Study Bible
[168] Romans 5:8b

forms. If anyone speaks, he should do it as one speaking the very words of God. If anyone serves, he should do it with the strength God provides, so that in all things God may be praised through Jesus Christ." (I Peter 4:9-11a, NIV)

Peter reminds us of our purpose: to glorify God in everything that we do . . . in everything we do, big things, and little things. And we have to start in the little things (like hospitality, speaking, serving).

That's why we're here.

And it has to start now.

And the words of the old hymn ring down through the years:

When My Love For Christ Grows Weak[169]
When my love for Christ grows weak
When for deeper faith I seek
Then in thought I go to thee
Garden of Gethsemane

There I walk amid the shade
Where the dwindling twilight fades
See the friendless lonely one
Weeping praying all alone

When my love for men grows weak
When for stronger faith I seek
Hill of Calvary I go
To your scenes of fear and woe

There I turn to life again
Learning all the worth of pain
Learning all the might that lies
In a full self-sacrifice

---

[169] Lyrics: John R. Wreford (1837); Music: Charles J. Vincent, Jr.; Public Domain

And I turn with firmer faith
To Christ who vanquished pain and death
And to Christ enthroned above
Raise a song of selfless love

"Does it make sense to pray for guidance about the future if we are not obeying in the thing that lies before us today? How many momentous events in Scripture depended on one person's seemingly small act of obedience! Rest assured: Do what God tells you to do now, and, depend upon it, you will be shown what to do next."[170]

"To Him be the glory and the power for ever and ever. Amen."
(I Peter 4:11b, NIV)

---

[170] Elisabeth Elliot (1926-2015)

??? QUESTIONS FOR REFLECTION

- Did the leaders ("elders") of the Amish community dishonor the memory of their daughters by such immediate forgiveness and grace?
- Is the spiritual condition of the perpetrator's survivors germane to the action of the victims' survivors?
- Could you have responded as the Amish?
- What is the most important thing?
  My happiness?
  Fairness?
  Justice?
  Revenge?
  My rights?
  My health?
  My life?
  The salvation of a soul from eternal death?

NINETEEN

THE BLESSING

First Peter 4:12-19

". . . they did not love their lives so
much as to shrink from death."
(Revelation 12:11b, NIV)

·· 19 ··

On June 17, 2015, Dylann Roof joined the Wednesday night Bible study at the Emanuel African Methodist Episcopal (AME) Church in Charleston, South Carolina. The young white man was welcomed into the predominantly black church and stayed through the time of study of Scripture. During the closing prayer, he pulled a gun, opened fire, and killed nine fellow members of the Bible class.

Two days later, survivors and relatives of the victims addressed Dylan. This is what they said.

"I forgive you; my family forgives you. We would like you to take this opportunity to repent. Repent. Confess. Give your life to the One who matters the most, Christ, so he can change your ways no matter what happens to you and you'll be OK. Do that and you'll be better off than you are right now."[171]

"We welcomed you Wednesday night in our Bible study with open arms. You have killed some of the most beautifulest people that I know. Every fiber in my body hurts...and I'll never be the same. Tywanza Sanders was my son, but Tywanza was my hero. Tywanza was my hero. But as we said in Bible study, we enjoyed you, but may God have mercy on you."[172]

"I forgive you. You took something really precious away from me. I will never talk to her ever again. I will never be able to hold her again. But I forgive you and have mercy on your soul. It hurts me, it hurts a lot of people but God forgive you and I forgive you."[173]

As Peter writes, it's almost as if he can hear the families of those around him. It's as if he can hear the voices of the survivors of those who had been killed for their faith.

And perhaps he had.

So, he encourages them. He reminds them. He wants them to know that this is normal. This is reality. This is the way things are in this world. They are on Satan's turf; after all, "the whole world is under the control of the evil one." (I John 5:19b, NIV) Their calling is to an alien world, one

---

[171] Anthony Thompson, representing family of Myra Thompson
[172] Felecia Sanders, mother of Tywanza Sanders
[173] Daughter of Ethel Lance

that is broken, fallen. It's a world that doesn't conform to the calling of their King, a call to selflessness.

"Dear friends, do not be surprised at the painful trial you are suffering, as though something strange were happening to you." (I Peter 4:12, NIV)

And nobody knows this better than Peter. He doesn't speak from a theoretical perspective. He doesn't speak as one who hasn't experienced similar suffering. Peter's been there, done that.

Not long after Pentecost, Peter and the other apostles were jailed for having violated the Sanhedrin's "strict orders not to teach in this name." (Acts 5:28, NIV) Sitting there that night in that public jail, none of them knew what awaited them. Humiliation? Beatings? Death? Peter had to be wondering, "Is this the day that I die?" But on this night, "an angel of the Lord opened the doors of the jail and brought them out," and told them to "Go, stand in the temple courts, and tell the people the full message of this new life." (Acts 5:20, NIV) So they did. Again. At daybreak.

Hauled before the Sanhedrin again, they were saved from death only by the wisdom of Gamaliel. But a flogging ensued. And yet, "the apostles left the Sanhedrin, rejoicing because they had been counted worthy of suffering disgrace for the Name." (Acts 5:41, NIV)

Peter got it. Peter knew suffering. Peter knew what it was to face death. And when he encourages his readers to "rejoice that you participate in the sufferings of Christ, so that you may be overjoyed when His glory is revealed" (I Peter 4:13, NIV), not only has he participated in Christ's sufferings, but he has seen Jesus's glory revealed through that suffering! He has seen that glory revealed both through Jesus' suffering, and through his own suffering. Peter doesn't have to wonder about the outcome.

Although he had not yet suffered unto death, Peter knew that "if you are insulted because of the name of Christ you are blessed, for the Spirit of glory and of God rests on you." (I Peter 4:14, NIV) He spoke from experience that "if you suffer as a Christian, do not be ashamed, but praise God that you bear that name." (I Peter 4:16, NIV)

Peter once again constrains us to rely on God. If we're going to obey Him, we must trust Him.

In the movie *Aladdin*, the title character and his girlfriend, Jasmine, are being pursued by her father's henchmen. Cornered on a perch high above the city, Aladdin asks Jasmine if she trusts him.

"What?!" exclaims Jasmine.

"Do you trust me?"

"Yes?" Jasmine responds, still with doubt in her voice.

"Then jump!" exclaims Aladdin.

God places the same question before us every day. "Do you trust Me?" But, unlike Aladdin, God is Creator. He created the universe. He created you. He created me. He created Peter and the Sanhedrin. He created Dylann Roof and the Emanuel AME Church.

He asked the same question of Noah, Abraham, and Moses. He asked it of the prophets. He asked it of John the Baptist. He asked them to do the same thing that the hymn writer admonishes.

Trust & Obey[174]

When we walk with the Lord
in the light of his word,
what a glory he sheds on our way!
While we do his good will,
he abides with us still,
and with all who will trust and obey.

Refrain:
Trust and obey, for there's no other way
to be happy in Jesus, but to trust and obey.

Not a burden we bear,
not a sorrow we share,
but our toil he doth richly repay;
not a grief or a loss,
not a frown or a cross,
but is blest if we trust and obey. [Refrain]

But we never can prove
the delights of his love
until all on the altar we lay;
for the favor he shows,

---

[174] John H. Sammis, 1887; Public Domain

for the joy he bestows,
are for them who will trust and obey. [Refrain]

Then in fellowship sweet
we will sit at his feet,
or we'll walk by his side in the way;
what he says we will do,
where he sends we will go;
never fear, only trust and obey.

God's either in control or He's not.

The night that Dylann Roof shared in the Word, the study was centered on Mark 4:16, in the middle of Jesus' parable of the seeds. The seed in verse 16 was sown on rocky places, emblematic of those who "hear the word and at once receive it with joy. But since they have no root, they last only a short time. **When trouble or persecution comes because of the Word, they quickly fall away.**" (Mark 4:16-17, NIV)

We don't know whether our brothers and sisters of Emanuel AME Church had studied First Peter. What we do know is that they lived it out. They recognized that "it is time for judgment to begin with the family of God; and if it begins with us, what will the outcome be for those who do not obey the gospel of God? And,

'If it is hard for the righteous to be
saved,
what will become of the ungodly and
the sinner?'"
(I Peter 4:17-18, NIV)

When trouble came because of the Word, they were not the "rocky places." They did not fall away. Not only did they not fall away, but they testified mightily for Peter when Jesus' glory was revealed in their words.

What they did was counter-cultural.

What they did was counter-intuitive.

What they did was counter-"common sense".

What they did was live out I Peter 4:19 (NIV) . . .

"So then, those who suffer according to God's will should commit themselves to their faithful Creator and continue to do good."

Just like Paul and Silas, when they were in Thessalonica in the first century, these brothers and sisters joined with them two thousand years later, and "turned the world upside down." (Acts 17:6, ESV)

Before a nation ready to witness resentment and hate, these Christians praised God that they bore His name. Before a broken world expecting spite and vengeance, the Spirit of glory and of God did indeed rest on them.

And that world, that nation wonders why?

⁇? QUESTIONS FOR REFLECTION

- Do *you* wonder why?
- If you had experienced the senseless murder of loved ones right before your eyes, could you respond as the Church in Charleston did? If not, why not? If so, how?
- Can Dylann Roof be saved? Is it possible that we could see him on the other side? Is anything else more important?
- So, who is your "Dylann Roof?"
- Does God cause suffering? (4:19) Or does God allow it?
- How does one act in the face of lying, cheating, betrayal, stealing, adultery, verbal abuse, physical abuse? How do I act toward the sinner (liar, cheater, betrayer, thief, adulterer, abuser)? If I act differently to one versus the other, am I not simply altering my response based on degree?

TWENTY

THE MEN

First Peter 5:1-7

"Maturity starts with the willingness to give oneself."[175]

[175] Elisabeth Elliot (1926-2015)

·· 20 ··

It began on March 23, 2018. Redouane Lakdim hijacked a car, killed a passenger and wounded the driver. Lakdim claimed ties to ISIS and was armed with a gun, a large hunting knife, and three explosive devices.

While fleeing in the stolen car, Lakdim fired his gun into a group of police officers, seriously injuring one of them. Then, he drove to Trèbes, a small town in the south of France. He barricaded himself into a grocery store with hostages.

A French police officer, Lt. Col. Arnaud Beltrame, 44, was one of the first to arrive at the scene. Beltrame already had a remarkable military career. Graduating at the top of his class from one of France's elite military schools, he was a member of an elite special forces unit in the French military. He had been decorated for service in Iraq.

He once again ran toward the sound of the guns, though this time it was in his native France. For a while it appeared that through his efforts there might be no more bloodshed. The terrorist released all the hostages but one, a woman named Julie. Then Lt. Col. Beltrame did a remarkable thing. He offered himself in exchange for Julie. Lakdim accepted the deal, and Beltrame laid down his weapons and entered the store. Julie came out unharmed.

Lt. Col. Arnaud Beltrame did not. What happened next is still a matter of some speculation, but shots rang out. The terrorist was killed, and Beltrame sustained bullet wounds in his arm and foot. But the fatal injury came from a severe knife wound to the neck. Beltrame died the next day.

Beltrame immediately and properly became a national hero. He was posthumously promoted to the rank of full colonel. At a funeral service broadcast on national television, Cedric Beltrame, Lt. Col. Beltrame's brother, said, "Beyond his job, he gave his life for someone else, for a stranger . . . he was well aware he had almost no chance. He was very aware of what he was doing . . . if we don't describe him as a hero, I don't know what you need to do to be a hero."

Beltrame was not raised in a religious home, but at the age of thirty-three he converted to Christianity. Dominique Arz, a chaplain in the national police who knew Beltrame said he "did not hide his faith, he radiated it. He went to the end of his service to the country and to the end of his testimony of faith. To believe is not only to adhere to a doctrine. It is first to love God and his neighbor, and to testify of his faith concretely in everyday life."

His pastor wrote "only his faith can explain the madness of this sacrifice, *which is today the admiration of all. I believe that only a Christian faith animated by charity could ask for this superhuman sacrifice."*[176]

As we listed relationship after relationship earlier:

- Citizen of a despot king
- Slave of an unjust master
- Executed Messiah of a mob
- Wife of an abusive husband
- Husband of an abusive wife,

Peter addresses "finally, all of you." (I Peter 3:8, NIV) But Peter wasn't really through. He reserved some more specifics for a couple of final categories, categories that he can identify with.

> "To the elders among you, I appeal as a fellow elder, a witness of Christ's sufferings and one who also will share in the glory to be revealed: Be shepherds of God's flock that is under your care, serving as overseers – not because you must, but because you are willing, as God wants you to be; not greedy for money, but eager to serve; not lording it over those entrusted to you, but being examples to the flock." (I Peter 5:1-3, NIV)

First, Peter singles out elders, appealing as a fellow elder, but then immediately identifying also with Jesus. (A "beeline to the cross?") What better way to appeal to his fellow elders than to remind them of Jesus' sufferings (and indirectly, Peter's denial). But then pivoting to sharing in Jesus' glory[177], Peter compels them to envision "**the most important thing!**"

Peter then puts the heavy responsibility on the elders to be shepherds and overseers. And with this calling to serve as shepherds and overseers comes the responsibility to serve as examples to the flock.[178]

---

[176] Warren Cole Smith, *Greater Love Hath No Man*, *Breakpoint*, March 30, 2018
[177] 5:1
[178] 5:3

Examples of what?

Yep. You guessed it.

This is simply the next in the line of Peter's list of "in the same ways" that point back to Jesus. (See above.) But this exhortation carries a special burden with it, the burden of leadership. And once again, his example is Jesus. Just as a captain is called to go down with his ship, so an elder is called to be the first to sacrifice. So, all of Peter's previous admonitions carry special significance for him and his fellow elders because they are to be the first to show the way for those in their flock.

First to submit.

First to be selfless.

First to serve.[179]

First to sacrifice.

First to suffer.

All the while pointing to the other side, to the only thing that will matter a hundred years from now. The crown.

> "And when the Chief Shepherd appears, you will receive the crown of glory that will never fade away." (I Peter 5:4, NIV)

In fact, it's the only thing that matters <u>now</u> to those that Peter was originally writing to!

"If you read history you will find that the Christians who did most for the present world were precisely those who thought most of the next. It is since Christians have largely ceased to think of the other world that they have become so ineffective in this."[180]

And in Peter's final "in the same way", he harkens the young men to submit to the elders . . . as they submit to Jesus.

"Young men, in the same way be submissive to those who are older." (I Peter 5:5a, NIV)

Keep in mind who this is that's writing! This is Peter. The young man, Peter? *Not* one to submit! *Not* one to be humble! And yet, he dovetails a call to humility onto his call to submission.

---

[179] 5:2

[180] *Mere Christianity*, C. S. Lewis

"All of you, clothe yourselves with humility toward one another, because, 'God opposes the proud but gives grace to the humble.'

Humble yourselves, therefore, under God's mighty hand, that He may lift you up in due time. Cast all your anxiety on Him because He cares for you." (I Peter 5:5b-7, NIV)

Wow! Pre-Pentecost "Peter the Proud" has truly become Post-Pentecost "Peter the Humble." And he shares his lessons, painful as they were, first to the young men, then to all . . . the lesson of submission.

?? QUESTIONS FOR REFLECTION

- What do I follow, "common sense" or Jesus?
- How do you make decisions?
- What (who) motivates you?
- What (who) inspires you?
- What (who) do you serve?
- What (who) controls you?
- Who is king/boss (Lord?) of your life?

TWENTY-ONE

THE FIGHT

First Peter 5:8-11

"Aim at heaven and you will get earth thrown in.
Aim at earth and you will get neither."[181]

---

[181] C. S. Lewis, *The Joyful Christian*

While imprisoned in Romania, Pastor Joseph Tson[182] told his captors, "Sir, let me explain how I see this issue. **Your supreme weapon is killing. My supreme weapon is dying.** *Here is how it works. You know that my sermons on tape have spread all over the country. If you kill me, those sermons will be sprinkled with my blood. Everyone will know I died for my preaching. And everyone who has a tape will pick it up and say, 'I'd better listen again to what this man preached, because he really meant it: he sealed it with his life.' So, sir, my sermons will speak 10 times louder than before. I will actually rejoice in this supreme victory if you kill me."*

You were wondering when it was going to happen, weren't you? You've been wondering if the old Peter would show up, right? After all, we said that Jesus didn't give Peter a personality transplant when He changed him! Well, here he is . . . but maybe in an unexpected way . . .

First, Peter identifies our enemy and describes his tactics.

> "Be . . . alert. Your enemy the devil prowls around like a roaring lion looking for someone to devour. Resist him, standing firm . . ." (I Peter 5:8-9a, NIV)

And he finally tells us to resist! Finally! No more submission, no more surrender, no more selflessness, no more sacrifice, right!?!?

Well, not exactly.

So, Peter, how do we resist our enemy? With guns? With fists? With violence?

Well, perhaps the clue to understanding how to fight one's enemy is to know the enemy's tactics. And in this case, what is it the enemy wants us to do?

Fight fire with fire! Eye for eye! Tooth for tooth!

"Then the whole world will be blind and toothless."[183]

---

[182] Former president of The Romanian Missionary Society in Wheaton, Illinois. Pastor of Second Baptist Church in Oradea, Romania until 1981, when he was exiled by the Romanian government.
[183] Tevye, "Fiddler on the Roof"

Instead, look at how Peter brackets his exhortations to "resist" and "stand firm": self-control and suffering.

> "Be self-controlled . . . because you know that your brothers throughout the world are undergoing the same kind of sufferings." (I Peter 5:8a, 9b, NIV)

Sound familiar?

And how do we do that? How, in the face of murder and mayhem, in the face of death and destruction, do we stand firm by controlling self and by suffering? Peter says, "I'm glad you asked that question."

> "And the God of all grace, Who called you to His eternal glory in Christ, after you have suffered a little while, will Himself restore you and make you strong, firm, and steadfast. To Him be the power forever and ever. Amen." (I Peter 5:10-11, NIV)

It is "the God of all grace" who will Himself empower you. It was He who called you to this mission. It was He who suffered. It was He who foresaw the suffering that *you* will endure. And it is He who "will make you strong, firm and steadfast."

And nobody knows this better than Peter.

Pre-Pentecost, he tried under the power of Peter. He used the strategy of Simon. He followed the wisdom of this world[184]. And he failed . . . miserably, defined by what he is not:

"I am not – this man's disciple.

I am not – destined for glory in a messianic kingdom.

I am not – the brave decisive right-hand man of my fond imagination."[185]

Post-Pentecost, Peter is a changed man. And he is still the strong man that we saw, pre-Pentecost. He now understands that true strength is exhibited by resisting the fleshly, human, "common sense" desires that he had previously succumbed to. And he and the other apostles have indeed

---

[184] I Corinthians 1:20
[185] Janie B. Cheaney, *Peter's Identity Crisis*, World Magazine, April 6, 2013

"turned the world upside down."[186] But by the power of the One who indwells them: the "I AM". And without a shot . . . without a sword . . . without the violence of the evil one.

The Hebrew writer reminded his recipients:

"Remember those earlier days after you had received the light, when you stood your ground in a great contest in the face of suffering. Sometimes you were publicly exposed to insult and persecution; at other times you stood side by side with those who were so treated. You sympathized with those in prison and joyfully accepted the confiscation of your property, because you knew that you yourselves had better and lasting possessions." (Hebrews 10:32-34, NIV)

They resisted. They stood firm.

So. Should. We.

---

[186] Acts 17:6 (ESV)

??? QUESTIONS FOR REFLECTION

- Was Pastor Tson a fool for taunting his captor to kill him? Does your knowledge of the outcome change your answer?
- Who/what am I to fight? Who is the enemy? How do I fight?
- Are you a gladiator or a spectator?
- Is there any sin that is <u>not</u> selfish?

TWENTY-TWO

THE TRUE GRACE

First Peter 5:12-14

"If you're born once, you have to die twice.
If you're born twice, you only have to die once."[187]

---

[187] Dr. David Jeremiah, Senior Pastor, Shadow Mountain Community Church

·· 22 ··

Early one morning, Will, the owner of a large manufacturing company, was greeted at his office door by his plant manager, John. Without comment, John was submitting his resignation, effective the following Friday. Will was devastated; for the past five years he had been grooming John to become president of the company.

When he questioned John about his reasons for leaving, John refused to discuss it. Will could not even begin to understand why John was leaving. He was paid more than anyone else in the company, including Will. But it was obvious that nothing was going to change John's mind. He had made the decision to leave.

Will asked John to stay long enough to hire and train a new plant manager, but he flatly refused and reacted angrily when Will asked. Since John had been such a good friend, Will held a company going-away party and gave John a substantial severance bonus.

Three months later, John's reasons for leaving became apparent when he opened his own company and copied Will's best-selling product. In time, John's company grew, and it became one of Will's leading competitors.

Nine years later, Will heard that there was a design problem with one of John's new products and that several lawsuits were being filed against John's company. Will had forgiven John years before and regularly prayed for him.

He felt strongly that the Lord wanted him to reach out to John, so he bought one of John's products, tested it, and discovered what the problem was. Will then put his engineers to work to correct the problem. After he made the necessary modifications and tested it, he called John and told him how to solve his problem.[188]

It's sign-off time. Time for Peter to land the plane. And boy, does he leave no doubt about his purpose.

He is "testifying that this is the true grace of God." (I Peter 5:12b, NIV)

So, we've finished the letter. What is "the true grace of God?"

In a word, selflessness. Remember? Pure, unadulterated, selflessness.

First.

Last.

---

[188] Larry Burkett, *Business by the Book*

Always.

In every situation.

Even to the giving of my life.

One has to wonder about Peter's thoughts as he penned this letter. As he spoke truth to those around him facing persecution, did he remember his denials? As he experienced the death of his brothers and sisters around him, did he wonder about his escape from his own death?

Was he thinking, "I haven't had to face death yet"?

Peter proclaimed to Jesus his willingness to die with and for Him.[189] But perhaps Peter was answering a question that Jesus wasn't asking of him. Although Peter eventually died for the Name, perhaps Jesus was really wanting to know if Peter would *live* for Him. Was that the question that was burned on Peter's mind when "the Lord turned and looked straight at"[190] him?

And this letter from our brother Peter compels me to be asked the question from Jesus, but which is He asking?

And which question is Jesus asking you today, dear Reader?

Will you live for Me?

Will you die for Me?

Both?

To die for Him will mean facing fear of the unknown, fear of the end of this life (the known).

To live for Him may mean facing other fears, fears that we've all experienced (the known). Fear of rejection. Fear of ostracization. Fear of humiliation. Fear of economic loss.

What about Will in the story above? Fool? Or servant of a crucified Savior living for Him?

Whichever question is being asked of us (and it may be both), God makes it clear that He is still on the throne. Abraham Kuyper[191] reminds us that "There is not a square inch in the whole domain of our human existence over which Christ, who is Sovereign over all, does not cry, Mine!" And God's most repeated **command** in Scripture is "Fear not!"

---

[189] Matthew 26:33
[190] Luke 22:61
[191] Prime Minister of The Netherlands, 1901-1905; Established the Reformed Churches in The Netherlands

And, because of this, Peter can sign off with peace for those of us who are in Christ . . . regardless . . . of life . . . or death.

"And so we follow God's own fool
For only the foolish can tell-
Believe the unbelievable
And come be a fool as well."[192]

---

[192] Michael Card, *"God's Own Fool"*

??? QUESTIONS FOR REFLECTION

- Was Will a fool? After all, "business is business."
- Could you have done as Will? If not, why not?
- We don't know what John's response was. Does it matter?
- Is there any sin that's not "all about me?"
- So, is there ever a time when I am <u>not</u> called to be a "doormat/push-over?" Is there a time when I am <u>not</u> called to abrogate my "rights" and instead, to "stand up for myself?"

EPILOGUE

"The passion of Christianity comes from deliberately signing away my own rights and becoming a bondservant of Jesus Christ. Until I do that, I will not begin to be a saint."[193]

---

[193] Oswald Chambers, *"My Utmost for His Highest"*

"'Is this the day I die?'
Simon Peter asked himself the familiar question
as he wiped sleep from his eyes."[194]

Yes, Peter, today is the day.

It's a day Jesus foresaw, a day set in time before time began.

Remember when He told you that when you are old you will stretch out your hands, and someone else will dress you and lead you where you do not want to go? You are old, Peter . . . and today is the day. Even now, they come to lead you. So, for now, Simon, son of Jonah, remember . . .

Remember when you first met Him? The catch of fish? The broken nets? The sinking boat?

And you left it all for Him.

You saw the dead raised, the blind see, the deaf hear, the lame walk, storms calmed, thousands fed . . . exciting times . . .

Remember walking on the sea? And only *you* got out of the boat! Ready for a sea of crystal? And then you sank, His hand reaching out to save you. That outstretched hand awaits again.

And remember your time on the mountain? Moses and Elijah? Bright as lightning? They're there, ready to see you again. But eyes have not seen the brightness of the glory of God that you're about to see.

Remember how you told the Messiah that you were ready to go to prison and to the death with Him? Well, prison is now behind you, Simon. Death is before you. And it is others who now stretch out your hands.

That Messiah knows how that feels.

But Peter, your head is down . . . bowed . . . you understand now . . . were you remembering His words, "A student is not above his teacher, nor a servant above his master?" (Matthew 10:24, NIV) Your final view of the world is upside down. So should it be. You understand clearly that His way is the way of the cross . . . death to self . . . the way of total surrender . . . total selflessness . . . total love . . . upside down from the ways of the world. Those who would crucify you appear to have the power. But, dear Peter, the words of your letter will ring across the ages. Little do they know that your death will be a seed that produces many seeds, and that the word of the Lord stands forever.

---

[194] With apologies to Randy Alcorn (See Introduction)

Do you remember the look in His eyes when the rooster crowed? You wept. Today, you will look into those eyes once more . . . but this time, tears of joy, impetuous Peter, tears of joy.

And remember Pentecost? They thought you were drunk! Oh, you were! But intoxicated with His Spirit . . . and you understood. It was then that you, Peter, the Rock, saw clearly and changed your view of the world. As you wrote in your letter to others not so long ago, 'to this you were called, because Christ suffered for you, leaving you an example, that you should follow in His steps.' Total selflessness.

The taste of your own blood is bitter as the end nears. It will soon be replaced. Remember at that first miracle, you got to taste for yourself that He always saves the best wine for last. Well, that taste now awaits you at His table.

Sleepy? You've been sleepy many times with Jesus before, Simon. Ah, but the sweetest sleep is the sleep that awaits.

You asked your Savior how many times you should forgive your brother when he sins against you. His Spirit has showed you what He meant by seventy times seven, has He not? And those that are doing this to you? This will be your final act of forgiveness. Oh, and Peter, you just might see some of them on the other side.

So, look to the sky and remember when you last saw Jesus. Ascending in the clouds. Come, take that journey and see Him again, Peter.

No more remembering now. Your yesterdays are gone. No more tomorrows. Only Eternity. You. And Jesus. Forever.

"Well done, good and faithful servant . . ."
(Matthew 25:21, NIV)

Soli

Deo

Gloria

Amen! and Amen!

APPENDIX

But what about . . .

OK. So, you've stayed with me through the entire book. Maybe you've been challenged to think about the call of Christ differently. Perhaps you've even looked on the past behavior of yourself and others, and seen a difference between that behavior and the behavior of Jesus, His disciples, and others whose stories you've now read about.

And it's challenged you.

But still . . . there are nagging doubts. Questions in your mind that "something just doesn't add up." Questions that start with "but what about?"

Yeah. Me, too.

When something goes against the grain as mightily as Jesus's calling, it grates against your deeply held beliefs. It flies in the face of human nature. It just doesn't "feel right." And there are certain specific instances where it just doesn't seem to fit.

After nearly thirty years and multiple classes and personal interactions around Peter's letter, there are four that seem to be predominant. I'll try to respond to them. I don't pretend to have all of the answers to even the four that I'm addressing here, much less others that you may think of. At the very least, perhaps this will provoke you to look at these differently than you have in the past.

So, please, read on.

JESUS IN THE TEMPLE?

Well, at the top of the list of seeming contradictions to what you've just read in this book has to be the episode of Jesus in the Temple.

So, let's take a look.

Any time I run onto a passage that seems to contradict all the other passages, then that single passage becomes the one that I concentrate on as being the one that I haven't rightly understood. The "cleansing of the temple" is just such a passage.

It seems to fly in the face of the Beatitudes.

It seems to fly in the face of the Sermon on the Mount.

It seems to fly in the face of the cross.

It seems to fly in the face of the apostolic letters (including First Peter) and the change that's reflected in the lives of the men that wrote them.

So, I have to ask, what is it about that episode that I don't understand? Does "the exception prove the rule?"

And I've read and contemplated that a long time. Here's all I've come up with at this point.

The cleansing/clearing of the temple appears to be an angry Jesus. I'm not one of those who would try to downplay Jesus' anger in the temple. Most of the commentaries I've read give Him His due for being angry and not sinning! (Actually, there may have even been two cleansings. John records it at the beginning of Jesus' ministry; the others record it at the end, almost as if it gives the appearance that Jesus has finally "had enough!" Most scholars think that John was totally unconcerned about chronology and totally concerned about message, and that they're talking about the same cleansing.) At any rate, what is the message?

Well, we have no physical temple now. We . . . you and I, are the temple, the dwelling place of God (the Holy Spirit). Paul expanded on this in First Corinthians when he said, "Don't you know that you yourselves are God's temple and that God's Spirit lives in you? If anyone destroys God's temple, God will destroy him; for God's temple is sacred, and you are that temple." (I Corinthians 3:16-17, NIV)

Jesus made it clear that this temple needs to be cleared of the worldly to make a place for the holy. The account in John is immediately followed by the Jews challenging His authority, to which He responded, "Destroy this temple, and I will raise it again in three days." (John 2:19, NIV) Of course, He was talking about His body.[195] This episode was not about Jesus' finally having reached a limit to His patience and losing His temper. This was about Jesus teaching that "My house will be called a house of prayer, but you are making it a den of robbers." (Matthew 21:13, NIV) It was about clearing out the worldly to make a place for the holy.

Jesus explained to the Samaritan woman at the well that "a time is coming when you will worship the Father neither on this mountain nor in Jerusalem." (John 4:21b, NIV) He taught that, "The kingdom of God does not come with your careful observation, nor will people say, 'Here it is' or 'There it is,' because the kingdom of God is within you." (Luke 17:20b-21, NIV)

It seems apparent that the temple cleansing of which Jesus spoke was not the one on the mountain in Jerusalem. It was my body; it is your body.

So, I guess the point is this. If something or somebody compels me to be angry, if I want to be frustrated, if I want to be impatient, if I want to be fed up, then it's my flesh that I should be angry, frustrated, impatient, or fed up with. It's me that I should want to "cleanse". It's my "temple" that I need to clear. It's my body from which I need to remove the profane to make way for the holy.

Let's take it a step further.

Do you have trouble understanding why Jesus singled out the money changers and those providing animals for sacrifice? After all, the reality is that they were providing a needed service to those who had traveled from long distances to Jerusalem. In fact, Jesus doesn't condemn them for what they did, only for where they did it. (Profiteering? Perhaps we imply that from Jesus' quote from Jeremiah about "a den of robbers.")[196] Do you wonder why He didn't show His wrath on those in charge (priests, scribes, Pharisees)? Why would He display His one outburst of wrath on some poor

---

[195] John 2:21
[196] Matthew 21:13, Jeremiah 7:11

merchants providing a service for worshippers (even if they happened to be making a profit)?

It appears that Jesus is giving a picture of a principle.

God's dwelling place (the Temple) is a holy place, set aside for Him. The principle is inescapable. We, our bodies (the dwelling places of God's Holy Spirit) are holy places set aside for Him. He wants them cleansed (just as He wanted the Temple in Jerusalem cleansed). If we want to be angry, if we want to display our wrath, if we have any righteous indignation, it needs to be directed toward our own bodies, our own selfishness, our own pride.

Because, you see, if this episode is all about Jesus becoming Popeye and saying, "That's all I can stands, I can't stands no more!", then there is no limit to when I can play the "temple" card. Fact is, I can play that card any time I want to be selfish. Period. End of story. I can call it righteous indignation, I can call it holy wrath, I can call it whatever I want. In the end, it's all about me.

And believe me, there are plenty of times that I would love to play that card.

Somebody hits me: "Jesus in the temple!"

Somebody cuts me off in traffic: "Jesus in the temple!"

Somebody disrespects me: "Jesus in the temple!"

Somebody cheats me: "Jesus in the temple!"

Somebody talks ugly to me: "Jesus in the temple!"

And when I say, "Jesus in the temple", I justify whatever behavior I want.

So please . . . please don't use that episode to justify your behavior when you've been wronged.

Tell me that you can't go on. I'm with you.

Tell me that your family can't be subject to someone who is an emotional wreck. I've got your back.

Tell me that your "temple" is in poor health and is suffering. I will pray for God to grant you healing.

But don't do it because you're ready to strike back. Don't do it because you're ready to teach somebody a lesson. Don't do it because you've weighed the balance of the cosmos and decided to become judge, jury, and executioner . . . meting out both compensatory and punitive punishment.

That's what Satan wants you to do.

It isn't what Jesus wants you to do . . . even as He was cleansing the Temple. That's not His nature.

And it's not the nature of God.

MY FAMILY?

What about defending my family? Do I sacrifice them or defend them?

Perhaps the distinctive here is a little simpler. Self versus others

In other words, if the question is one of my selfish needs, desires, or well-being, then the principle of self-sacrifice applies. On the other hand, if the question is one of defending others, we are called to "defend the cause of the weak and fatherless" (Psalm 82:3a, Isaiah 1:17, NIV) and "rescue the weak and needy." (Psalm 82:4, NIV) The call is one to defend others, especially those who are unable to defend themselves.

Such is the picture Paul paints when he points to the rarity of "someone dying for a righteous man." (Romans 5:7, NIV) In reality, it reinforces the sacrificial love of Jesus referenced again and again by Peter in his letter.

In fact, stories shared in the book reinforce this principle:

- Lt. Col. Arnaud Beltrame sacrificing his life for Julie
- Ernest Gordon's fellow soldier sacrificing his life for his fellow soldiers

NATIONS?

OK. So, what about nations? Are nations supposed to just lay down and roll over? Are we all supposed to become like Switzerland and be neutral? Should we not defend ourselves? And what about those of us in the States who are descendants and beneficiaries of the American Revolution? I mean, after all, it was a *revolution* against a state, a nation, an authority that God presumably had put in place.[197] And, by all historical accounts, these were Godly men who fostered and led that revolution? And what about the Israelite nation being told to destroy every man, woman, child, and animal in the cities they conquered?

Great questions.

Perhaps the first principle that may help us navigate this thorny issue is articulated in a quote from American founding father George Mason:

"As nations cannot be rewarded or punished in the next world, they must be in this. By an inevitable chain of causes and effects, Providence punishes national sins with national calamities."[198]

And let's start with the last question first. What about Israel and God's command to them to totally destroy everything in Canaan?

As we've hinted at previously, for every principle in the New Testament, there is a picture in the Old Testament. And this picture of Israel is entirely consistent with what we discussed previously regarding the cleansing of the Temple by Jesus. God is holy. His people are holy. And in this picture of Israel, God is cleansing the Promised Land of the profane to make way for the holy.

And how profane the inhabitants of the Promised Land were.

As is well-known, the Canaanites worshiped idols. What may not be as well-known is what this worship involved. Was it simply bowing down to a statue of wood or metal? Yes, but there was more . . . so much more. For

---

[197] Romans 13:1
[198] Debate in the Federal Convention . . . condemning slavery, August 22, 1787

their worship involved orgies and child sacrifice. And to them (an agrarian culture), it made perfect sense.

They worshiped Baal, their god of thunder, lightning, and rain. He is portrayed in statues with a lightning bolt in his fist raised above his head. It was he who brought the rain that caused their crops to flourish and made the economy grow and the nation prosper. Baal's consort was Asherah (or Ashtoreth), portrayed in statues as multi-breasted. Their concept tied the fertility of the country with the fertility of their gods. So, if Baal and Asherah could be induced to copulate, favorable weather would ensue, resulting in good crops, fertile herds, and a good economy.

Hence, the orgies, complete with shrine prostitutes to help the festivities along. Sex by the worshippers induced sex by their gods, which led to the fertility of the land and the herds.

Add to that, Molech.

The god Molech was depicted with a bull's head and outstretched arms with palms turned upward in expectation and presumption of a sacrifice. Once again, the fertility of the wombs of the flocks and herds (the basis of their economy) was tied to the fertility of the wombs of the worshippers. Hence, the brass arms of the idol were heated by fire from beneath, and human infants (the product of the womb) were placed on Molech's arms as a sacrifice for a better economy.[199]

Makes perfect sense, huh? After all, "it's the economy . . . !"[200] (Right?)

And so, God cleansed this profanity to make way for His holiness. He cleared the licentiousness and rebellion of the Canaanites to allow His holiness to reign. He was placing His people, Israel, at the crossroads of the world that the world would know Him through them. And He knew that their fleshly nature would be drawn to the enticement of a worship tied to sexual pleasure and a preponderance of this world's goods. So, they were told to totally destroy the occupants of the land.

Israel did not comply. They didn't cleanse the land, and they were, indeed, drawn away from Yahweh and fell into the same trap that our current Sexual Revolution has set for us in the twenty-first century.

---

[199] And are we any different? We sacrifice our children on the altar of abortion because of the cost of the child (either directly to our pocketbooks, or to our loss of freedom to pursue an education or career: our economy).

[200] James Carville, Campaign Manager, 1992 Presidential Campaign, Bill Clinton

And then there's the American Revolution.

In addition to the earlier quote from George Mason, perhaps the best response to how a revolution could be justified would come from The Declaration of Independence. After all, why was such a document needed in the first place? If the colonies wanted to throw off the yoke of the government of Great Britain, why not just ignore their edicts and laws and make their own? Well, they knew the seriousness of their actions. They knew the gravity of their rebellion against authority.

And so, as they rebelled, they put pen to paper and wrote that "a decent respect to the opinions of mankind requires that they should declare the causes which impel them to the separation." They then stated that rights were derived, not from another person, but from the Creator. And that whatever powers any government might have were derived "from the consent of the governed." After declaring that the King of Great Britain had abused the power given to him, they then set out to prove his abuse, via "facts submitted to a candid world."

They then closed their Declaration by "appealing to the Supreme Judge of the world for the rectitude of our intentions", and stating "a firm reliance on the protection of Divine Providence."

In other words, they did not take their actions lightly. And to that extent, they believed that God would judge and act on their actions. If they were justified in their rebellion, He would act in their favor; if not, they would fail . . . again, acting as a nation understanding that the consequences would incur in this life since there was no "afterlife" for the nation to be judged in.

THE DEATH PENALTY?

This question is one that stokes strong emotions on both sides of the issue. Many people of high respect and integrity point back to the Noahic covenant in Genesis 9:4-6. God segues from giving animals to man to eat (but forbidding eating of the lifeblood) to the lifeblood of man.

> "But you must not eat meat that has its lifeblood still in it.
> And for your lifeblood I will surely demand an accounting.
> I will demand an accounting from every animal. And
> from each man, too, I will demand an accounting for the
> life of his fellow man.
>
> Whoever sheds the blood of man,
> by man shall his blood be shed;
> for in the image of God
> has God made man."
> (Genesis 9:4-6, NIV)

This is not a topic with which I am unfamiliar. In 1970, when I was seventeen years old, my grandmother was murdered in a botched burglary. Beatrice "Bea" Clay was a community icon. Named Durant's "Woman of the Year", Grandmother was serving on the U. S. President's Committee on Hiring the Handicapped and an identical state committee for Governor Bartlett at the time of her death. Sunday School teacher for over forty years, she served as President of three local service organizations. She adopted a nephew when her sister and brother-in-law died; that seven year old orphan grew up to become my father.

Her murderer left quite a different legacy. In 1970, John Loren Taylor pled guilty to a bogus check charge and was released after drawing a two-year suspended sentence. He was returned to jail a few days later after stealing a car, but the DA declined to press an application to revoke his suspended sentence and he was again released. Three days later, he murdered my Grandmother.

Mr. Taylor was sentenced to life imprisonment and three one-hundred-year sentences. All four sentences were to be served consecutively. He successfully escaped from prison once, and I still well remember the fear in my family and our community.

After the passing of my uncle and my father, the responsibility fell to me to monitor and manage our family's response to Mr. Taylor's imprisonment. I made multiple successful appeals to the Oklahoma Pardon and Parole Board to deny any parole for my Grandmother's murderer.

So, my thoughts may surprise you. But they may not.

It all boils down to the question that titles this book: what is **the most important thing**?

And while there is no specific passage addressing capital punishment in the New Testament, the answer to our recurring question may provide some guidance. After all, the answer to the question, the most important thing for any human being (all made in the image of God) is that we see that person on the other side.

That can only happen through saving faith in the Savior, Jesus, the Christ.

And arriving at that faith can only occur while one is alive.

In other words, as long as there is life, there is hope.

Perhaps there is no better example than that of Saul, "circumcised on the eighth day, of the people of Israel, of the tribe of Benjamin, a Hebrew of Hebrews; in regard to the law, a Pharisee; as for zeal, persecuting the church; as for legalistic righteousness, faultless." (Philippians 3:5-6, NIV) And yet, Saul, the murderer (by complicity if not explicitly) became Paul, the apostle.

What an incredible testimony to the changing power of the Gospel of Christ!

So, could the same thing happen to Dylann Roof? One by one, the survivors from Emanuel AME Church spoke in terms of praying for the confessed murderer to repent, and for God to have mercy on his soul. Although alive at the time of this writing, he has been sentenced to death.

Or what about Jeffery Dahmer, confessed murderer of at least sixteen men in the 1980s. At the time, Dahmer's crimes were considered some of the most heinous known. Because his state did not have the death penalty, Dahmer was sentenced to multiple life sentences. While in prison, he asked for a Bible, was born again, and baptized two years after his confinement. He later was beaten to death by a fellow prisoner. Will we see him on the other side? What if he had been executed before his conversion?

And what about John Loren Taylor?

I don't know.

I have few regrets in life, but one such regret is that I did not take the opportunity to connect personally with Mr. Taylor to forgive and share Jesus with him before his passing in prison on July 10, 2015. I regret that I did not make the opportunity to be sure of his status in regard to **the most important thing**.

It is now too late.

Printed in the United States
by Baker & Taylor Publisher Services